PLOT *your* WORK

STANDARD 5 EDITION

THE WRITER'S PROJECT PLANNER

Designed by C.J. Ellisson

Red Hot Publishing
P.O. BOX 651193, STERLING VA, 20165-1193

Standard Edition, Wire-Bound Format ISBN 978-1-938601-378
Standard Edition, Workbook/Perfect Bound Format ISBN 978-1-938601-583

This Planner Belongs To: _____

If Found, Please Call or Text: _____

Or eMail/Mail To: _____

_____

Suggested Use for Standard and Expanded Editions

PLOT
your
WORK

THE WRITER'S PROJECT PLANNER

Welcome to the project planner that will transform your organizational habits and productivity efforts! We created this tool to aid in your **existing** creative and business processes, *not* to teach you how to use a new "system," so creating instructions for how to use the planner was a bit tricky.

Take a look at the contents and skim through the pages. You'll see a lot of them are blank. Before you panic, think about why you bought this planner. You know how to plot a book, develop characters, research your setting, and create extensive world-building. You're already published, or close to it, and you know what it takes to market, promote, distribute, and everything else associated with being a professional writer. This planner was not intended to teach you how to do any of the above tasks.

If you're like us, the real problem has been in finding a product where we could manage *all* the various aspects of our work in one place—*and* for more than one project.

Are you a data-numbers type of person with extensive spreadsheets on sales, ROI, and ranking? Keep using those sheets; to give them up would mean committing yourself to lots of hand-written tracking. Some things are better tracked online, and others you need to see visually, on paper, not only for easy reference, but also to keep it in the forefront of your mind.

In using this planner, you're essentially creating several mini-business plans for multiple products—which is exactly what writing and releasing more than one book a year is.

In the first section, you'll map out the big picture in **Yearly Overview**. Starting with the first yearly spread, fill in the names of the months and add pertinent dates from your existing work and personal calendar, like deadlines, vacations, writing conferences, writing retreats, reader conventions, book signings, known obligations—and you'll include a "release date window" of time for new releases, to give yourself flexibility as you grow toward becoming more disciplined with staying on track. There are also two dot-grid pages after each yearly spread to expand on plans as needed.

Project Planning Pages:

First, make a list of everything you do for *every* book—or look over the **Sample Task List** we provide on each project spread and see what's missing from your current process. Do you revise four times before sending to your editor? Or do you let an MS sit for a few weeks and then come back to it? Add whatever YOU need to the checklist space at the bottom.

The following Sample Tasks are meant to **assist** in filling out a project plan. The suggestions are not meant to alter your existing processes:

- ☐ Brainstorm
- ☐ Character Sketches
- ☐ Research
- ☐ Begin Plot
- ☐ Finish Plot
- ☐ Compose Full Outline
- ☐ Write Book Description
- ☐ Send to Alpha Readers
- ☐ Revise again
- ☐ Send to Editor
- ☐ Incorporate Edits & Revisions

Title: *Dalton's Revenge*   Projected MS Length: *70k*

Pick a reward (Treat Yo' Self) for completing this project: *Weekend hiking in She*

First Quarter

week	October	month 1
1	*Research Setting*	
2	*Develop Characters*	
3	*Brainstorm plot, Begin Outline*	
4	*Finish Outline, start scene planning*	
5		

Second Quarter

week	January	
1	*Send to Edito*	
2	*Write Blurb*	
3	*Incorporate Send to pr*	
5		

Now, using a pencil, pick an upcoming novel you've yet to release, and fill out your work schedule in the first project spread. This is the place for big picture stuff. When you list something like "Edit Book," you could later break that down to weekly and daily goals.

Another task, like "Order Cover," isn't like ordering a pizza—one click and you're done. Sometimes you have to research a new artist, bid with several for a concept, review drafts, make suggestions, or get on a preferred contractor's wait list because they're busy. These smaller tasks will come into play with the Three Month Goal Planner.

Lined & Dot-grid Pages:

Use these pages for anything you need. Get creative!

If you've got an upcoming sale planned and want to track results, use a ruler and create a table with your stats.

Did you send out a contest entry or publisher submission and don't need a spreadsheet to track five or six items? Then make your own list with dates and follow-up information.

Are you looking to design a marketing plan for your next release? Check out marketing books and industry blogs related to selling books to help you devise a strategy that will work for your genre or topic—and use this planner to map it all out.

Do you like to mind-map your ideas? Try turning the notebook to the side, so the coils run along the top, and scribble away.

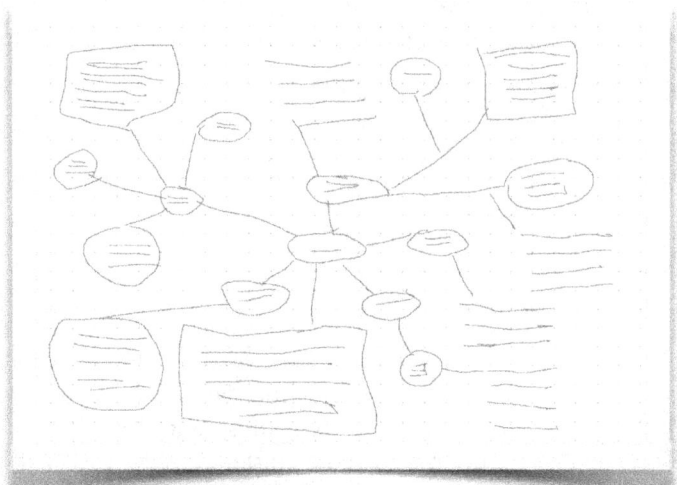

How about a review of your plot points? Draw a plot rollercoaster and fill it in.

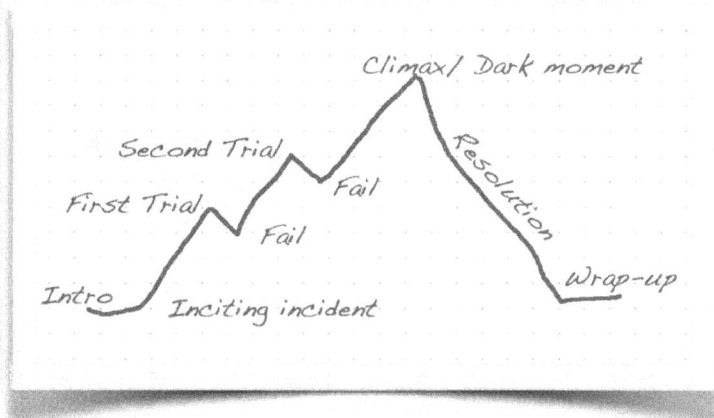

The possibilities with unscripted pages are endless. If we'd inserted a character sketch page with detailed prompts, or a plot diagram, you might be annoyed there were pages you couldn't use.

> **One bit of advice**: While we designed this tool to organize the business side of writing, we used it for creative aspects, too. It's your planner; do with it what you want, but please don't expect to plot out an entire book *and* all needed business tasks* in **one** section. Unless you plot loosely, there might not be enough space to do both.
>
> *If that is your goal, you may benefit from an edition with fewer project spreads and more pages per project, like the Deluxe + Scene Planning Edition.*

Next, repeat what you just did for each project you intend to work on this year. If it's more than five, you may want to consider the Scene Planning Edition of the Writer's Project Planner. It doesn't contain the below accountability & tracking sections, but it does have room to map out work on nine projects. If you're a high-productivity author you may not need the extensive tracking tools found in this edition.

Three Month Goal Planning:

Now that you have a grasp on the big picture for several projects, let's narrow the scope to what needs to be done over the next quarter. Review each project's first quarter and transfer the listed items to this page. This is where you'll break larger ones down to manageable chunks.

As an example, if you were to list "Revise Manuscript," that's a pretty big job. How many pages can you do per day, or week? Then list the revision process as an ongoing goal with several cumulative tasks dedicated to completing it.

Monthly Prioritizing:

After planning out your tasks for the quarter, you'll break down what needs to be done first. When creating task lists, the items aren't always written in the order they need to be completed. This is where you look at your upcoming work and prioritize which tasks need to be done immediately.

Quarterly Project Planning

Three Month Goal Planner
into concrete goals, check off when complete. Try not

Goal: *Revise DR*	Goal:
Project: *DR*	Proje
Due Date: *12/1*	Due I
Tasks to complete this Goal:	Task:
□1 *Character Analysis*	□1
□2 *GMC each chapter*	□2
□3 *Flow & Pacing*	□3
□4 *Line edits*	□4
□5 *Story Continuity*	□5

First 30 Days
Look over tasks from the Three Month Planner, and list below one to two
Adjust to these new organizational methods and stay on track. Completin
overwhelmed.

Quarterly Goal Focus Items for Next 30 Days:

Research Bk 2 □	*Develop Characrters* □	*Edit chp 1-5*
Cover Bk 2 □	*Write 10k* □	*Write 1C*
Get on Editor's schedule □	*Work on NL* □	*Send NL*

Social Media Planning Pages:

Are you tired of scrambling at the last minute to post relevant, engaging content? Well, what if you planned ahead and scheduled your posts? We primarily use Facebook to engage readers, but the same organizational tactics can be used on *any* social media network.

How do you figure out what to post? We give suggestions on relevant content in the Business Growth Idea for 1st QTR, Month 1, Week 4. The advice is simple, but it puts you on the right path.

Social Media Planning *FB* — Second Quarter — Mon

Monthly Planner for: ___*FB*___ (which Social Media account)   Day(s) to Sc

What to post and when. Schedule ahead! Check project calendars first, then add the relevant post targeted audience content, things that make you laugh, or share posts from your newsfeed that ca think your readers might enjoy.   *Check next to day when you've scheduled the post

-> Interior columns can be used for multiple accounts, multiple posts, or ignored. Use only

Date	Type of Post(s)	
□3/20	*Redheads Rule w/pic*	
□3/21	*Dog Pic*	*re-share on Instagram*
□3/22	*Sale on Dalton's Fury*	*re-post*

Weekly Action Plans:

By now, you're probably wondering why you're writing the same tasks over and over again in another place, but hold on —there is a method to the madness. It's been proven if you write something down several times it "sticks" in your mind. Can you think of a better way to engrave the importance of your work into the forefront of your thoughts?

Write. It. Down. Seriously.

With each stroke of your pen, you commit to your writing-related tasks and goals. Give it a try. All you've got to lose is a few minutes of your time.

In these planning pages, you'll not only list your weekly focus items, you'll also find inspirational quotes and business growth ideas for all types of writers. Some of it you may already know, but maybe a few ideas will be new to you.

Top Three Focus Items from Monthly Breakdown: | Are you feeling strong?

Edit Chapters 1-5 | *Write 10k!!* | *Start NL*

Weekly Action Plan: *Add to your regular weekly planner/agenda
Besides your daily writing time, what else do you need to accomplish? Admin work, cover design, editing, research? Block ti then be realistic with what you can handle daily. Check your regular agenda and remember to schedule time for you.

Monday: *Write 2.5k, edit chp 1*

Tuesday: *Write 2.5k, edit chp 2, find pics to post on FB*

Wednesday: *Edit chp 3 & 4, scene plan in afternoon*

Once your weekly tasks are mapped out, transfer the upcoming items to your regular planner, and put this planner away 'til next week. **Do not obsess.** Give yourself space & time to **work, focus, and create.**

Additionally, this edition has extensive tracking space available, with prompts at the end of each month and quarterly reviews. Use them or ignore them, it's up to you and what *you* need for your business.

For those of you who hate to read instructions:

1) **Yearly Overview:** Use your regular planner in addition to this one, it's not meant as a daily-use planner. Include any obligations that are important. Be aware of them as you plan the rest of your work.

2) **Project Planning:** Know your title, projected word count, how many words you can **consistently** write per day, and your release date window. Work back from your release date or plan forward based on words per day written. And include EVERYTHING you need to publish and publicize your book.

3) **Three Month Goals:** Where you map out what needs to be done over the next three months, based on what you filled in for your project planning. Bigger project tasks get broken down further in this step.

4) **Monthly Prioritizing:** One step further, dividing tasks from the three month plan to the next month, and the one after that, and the one after that…. you get the drift. You're smart. You're a writer.

5) **Weekly Action Plans:** Mapping out tasks you need to do weekly to stay on track with all your project goals. Don't try to be Wonder Woman just yet. Learn to work your plan. Stay on track. Learn your limits. Find balance.

See? Simple. It's not rocket science. You wrote a book. If you can plot a well-crafted story that engages your readers, you sure as hell can **Plot Your Work.**

You've got this. Go forth and create!

**There's also a Facebook group for Plot Your Work. If interested in joining, you can find it at this web address:
https://www.facebook.com/groups/PlotYourWork/

Customizable Table of Contents

2018

January
S	M	T	W	T	F	S
	1	2	3	4	5	6
7	8	9	10	11	12	13
14	15	16	17	18	19	20
21	22	23	24	25	26	27
28	29	30	31			

February
S	M	T	W	T	F	S
				1	2	3
4	5	6	7	8	9	10
11	12	13	14	15	16	17
18	19	20	21	22	23	24
25	26	27	28			

March
S	M	T	W	T	F	S
				1	2	3
4	5	6	7	8	9	10
11	12	13	14	15	16	17
18	19	20	21	22	23	24
25	26	27	28	29	30	31

April
S	M	T	W	T	F	S
1	2	3	4	5	6	7
8	9	10	11	12	13	14
15	16	17	18	19	20	21
22	23	24	25	26	27	28
29	30					

May
S	M	T	W	T	F	S
		1	2	3	4	5
6	7	8	9	10	11	12
13	14	15	16	17	18	19
20	21	22	23	24	25	26
27	28	29	30	31		

June
S	M	T	W	T	F	S
					1	2
3	4	5	6	7	8	9
10	11	12	13	14	15	16
17	18	19	20	21	22	23
24	25	26	27	28	29	30

July
S	M	T	W	T	F	S
1	2	3	4	5	6	7
8	9	10	11	12	13	14
15	16	17	18	19	20	21
22	23	24	25	26	27	28
29	30	31				

August
S	M	T	W	T	F	S
			1	2	3	4
5	6	7	8	9	10	11
12	13	14	15	16	17	18
19	20	21	22	23	24	25
26	27	28	29	30	31	

September
S	M	T	W	T	F	S
						1
2	3	4	5	6	7	8
9	10	11	12	13	14	15
16	17	18	19	20	21	22
23/30	24	25	26	27	28	29

October
S	M	T	W	T	F	S
	1	2	3	4	5	6
7	8	9	10	11	12	13
14	15	16	17	18	19	20
21	22	23	24	25	26	27
28	29	30	31			

November
S	M	T	W	T	F	S
				1	2	3
4	5	6	7	8	9	10
11	12	13	14	15	16	17
18	19	20	21	22	23	24
25	26	27	28	29	30	

December
S	M	T	W	T	F	S
						1
2	3	4	5	6	7	8
9	10	11	12	13	14	15
16	17	18	19	20	21	22
23/30	24/31	25	26	27	28	29

2019

January
S	M	T	W	T	F	S
		1	2	3	4	5
6	7	8	9	10	11	12
13	14	15	16	17	18	19
20	21	22	23	24	25	26
27	28	29	30	31		

February
S	M	T	W	T	F	S
					1	2
3	4	5	6	7	8	9
10	11	12	13	14	15	16
17	18	19	20	21	22	23
24	25	26	27	28		

March
S	M	T	W	T	F	S
					1	2
3	4	5	6	7	8	9
10	11	12	13	14	15	16
17	18	19	20	21	22	23
24	25	26	27	28	29	30

April
S	M	T	W	T	F	S
	1	2	3	4	5	6
7	8	9	10	11	12	13
14	15	16	17	18	19	20
21	22	23	24	25	26	27
28	29	30				

May
S	M	T	W	T	F	S
			1	2	3	4
5	6	7	8	9	10	11
12	13	14	15	16	17	18
19	20	21	22	23	24	25
26	27	28	29	30	31	

June
S	M	T	W	T	F	S
						1
2	3	4	5	6	7	8
9	10	11	12	13	14	15
16	17	18	19	20	21	22
23/30	24	25	26	27	28	29

July
S	M	T	W	T	F	S
	1	2	3	4	5	6
7	8	9	10	11	12	13
14	15	16	17	18	19	20
21	22	23	24	25	26	27
28	29	30	31			

August
S	M	T	W	T	F	S
				1	2	3
4	5	6	7	8	9	10
11	12	13	14	15	16	17
18	19	20	21	22	23	24
25	26	27	28	29	30	31

September
S	M	T	W	T	F	S
1	2	3	4	5	6	7
8	9	10	11	12	13	14
15	16	17	18	19	20	21
22	23	24	25	26	27	28
29	30					

October
S	M	T	W	T	F	S
		1	2	3	4	5
6	7	8	9	10	11	12
13	14	15	16	17	18	19
20	21	22	23	24	25	26
27	28	29	30	31		

November
S	M	T	W	T	F	S
					1	2
3	4	5	6	7	8	9
10	11	12	13	14	15	16
17	18	19	20	21	22	23
24	25	26	27	28	29	30

December
S	M	T	W	T	F	S
1	2	3	4	5	6	7
8	9	10	11	12	13	14
15	16	17	18	19	20	21
22	23	24	25	26	27	28
29	30	31				

Yearly Overview
Additional Notes:

Your Year at a Glance   This is where you map out all your known obligations for the coming year.

First Quarter

week   month 1

1 ....

2 ....

3 ....

4 ....

5 ....

....

week   month 2

1 ....

2 ....

3 ....

4 ....

5 ....

....

week   month 3

1 ....

2 ....

3 ....

4 ....

5 ....

....

Notes

....

....

....

....

....

....

....

Second Quarter

week   month 4

1 ....

2 ....

3 ....

4 ....

5 ....

....

week   month 5

1 ....

2 ....

3 ....

4 ....

5 ....

....

week   month 6

1 ....

2 ....

3 ....

4 ....

5 ....

....

Notes

....

....

....

....

....

....

....

Yearly Overview

Like family plans, weddings, work trips, birthdays, holidays, and vacations, that kind of thing. Not your writing stuff.

Third Quarter

week	month 7
1	
2	
3	
4	
5	

week	month 8
1	
2	
3	
4	
5	

week	month 9
1	
2	
3	
4	
5	

Notes

Fourth Quarter

week	month 10
1	
2	
3	
4	
5	

week	month 11
1	
2	
3	
4	
5	

week	month 12
1	
2	
3	
4	
5	

Notes

Yearly Overview
Notes, Mind Mapping, Bullet Journaling, Doodling, or To-Do Lists:

© Plot Your Work

Next Twelve Months

First Quarter

Second Quarter

....

....

....

....

....

....

....

....

....

....

....

....

....

....

....

....

....

....

Third Quarter

Fourth Quarter

....

....

....

....

....

....

....

....

....

....

....

....

....

....

....

....

....

....

Title:_____   **Projected MS Length:** _____   **Words Per Day:**_____

Pick a reward (Treat Yo' Self) for completing this project: _____

First Quarter

week   month 1

1

2

3

4

5

week   month 2

1

2

3

4

5

week   month 3

1

2

3

4

5

Second Quarter

week   month 4

1

2

3

4

5

week   month 5

1

2

3

4

5

week   month 6

1

2

3

4

5

The following Sample Tasks are meant to **assist** in filling out a project plan, the suggestions are **not** meant to alter your existing processes:

- ☐ Brainstorm
- ☐ Character Sketches
- ☐ Research
- ☐ Begin Plot
- ☐ Finish Plot
- ☐ Compose Full Outline
- ☐ Create Map
- ☐ Create Timeline
- ☐ Set Word Count per day
- ☐ Write First Draft
- ☐ Write Synopsis
- ☐ Self-edit
- ☐ Revise
- ☐ Edit via Program or App

- ☐ Write Book Description
- ☐ Send to Alpha Readers
- ☐ Revise again
- ☐ Send to Editor
- ☐ Incorporate Edits & Revisions
- ☐ Send to Beta Readers
- ☐ Revise/Edit again
- ☐ Submit to Agent
- ☐ Submit to Publisher
- ☐ Send to Proofreader
- ☐ Final Pass Before Format
- ☐ Research Cover Artists
- ☐ Order Cover: **eBook / Print**

- ☐ Finalize Cover
- ☐ Schedule Cover Reveal
- ☐ Format eBook (Self)
- ☐ Send to Formatter
- ☐ Galley Edits
- ☐ Format Print (Self)
- ☐ Inspect Finals
- ☐ Upload Files for Pre-order
- ☐ Contact Reviewers
- ☐ Develop Marketing Plan
- ☐ Sale on Backlist
- ☐ Send Updates to Newsletter
- ☐ Update Website

- ☐ Write/Send Press Release
- ☐ Research Email Services
- ☐ Order Promotional Material
- ☐ Contact Advertisers
- ☐ Compose Ad Copy
- ☐ Buy/Create Ad Images
- ☐ Schedule Ads
- ☐ Schedule Social Media Posts
- ☐ Update Backmatter Buy-links
- ☐ Upload Final Files
- ☐ Claim Title: Amazon/Bookbub
- ☐ Release Day Newsletter Push
- ☐ Schedule Reader Contests

       © **Plot Your Work**

Duration to Write:_____ **Release Date:**_____ ☐ **In Production**   ☐ **WiP**   ☐ **Done**

Progress Meter:
(fill in for each 10% completed)

| | | | | | | | | | | |

Third Quarter

week	month 7
1	
2	
3	
4	
5	

week	month 8
1	
2	
3	
4	
5	

week	month 9
1	
2	
3	
4	
5	

Additional Tasks:

☐   ☐

☐   ☐

☐   ☐

☐   ☐

☐   ☐

☐   ☐

☐   ☐

☐   ☐

Fourth Quarter

week	month 10
1	
2	
3	
4	
5	

week	month 11
1	
2	
3	
4	
5	

week	month 12
1	
2	
3	
4	
5	

Notes

© **Plot Your Work**

Notes, Marketing Plan, Character Sketches, World Building, Mind Mapping, Bullet Journaling, Doodling, or To-Do Lists:

Yearly Project Planning   **Project Two**

Title:_____ **Projected MS Length:** _____ **Words Per Day:**_____

Pick a reward (Treat Yo' Self) for completing this project: _____

First Quarter

week	month 1
1	
2	
3	
4	
5	

week	month 2
1	
2	
3	
4	
5	

week	month 3
1	
2	
3	
4	
5	

Second Quarter

week	month 4
1	
2	
3	
4	
5	

week	month 5
1	
2	
3	
4	
5	

week	month 6
1	
2	
3	
4	
5	

The following Sample Tasks are meant to **assist** in filling out a project plan, the suggestions are **not** meant to alter your existing processes:

- ☐ Brainstorm
- ☐ Character Sketches
- ☐ Research
- ☐ Begin Plot
- ☐ Finish Plot
- ☐ Compose Full Outline
- ☐ Create Map
- ☐ Create Timeline
- ☐ Set Word Count per day
- ☐ Write First Draft
- ☐ Write Synopsis
- ☐ Self-edit
- ☐ Revise
- ☐ Edit via Program or App

- ☐ Write Book Description
- ☐ Send to Alpha Readers
- ☐ Revise again
- ☐ Send to Editor
- ☐ Incorporate Edits & Revisions
- ☐ Send to Beta Readers
- ☐ Revise/Edit again
- ☐ Submit to Agent
- ☐ Submit to Publisher
- ☐ Send to Proofreader
- ☐ Final Pass Before Format
- ☐ Research Cover Artists
- ☐ Order Cover: **eBook / Print**

- ☐ Finalize Cover
- ☐ Schedule Cover Reveal
- ☐ Format eBook (Self)
- ☐ Send to Formatter
- ☐ Galley Edits
- ☐ Format Print (Self)
- ☐ Inspect Finals
- ☐ Upload Files for Pre-order
- ☐ Contact Reviewers
- ☐ Develop Marketing Plan
- ☐ Sale on Backlist
- ☐ Send Updates to Newsletter
- ☐ Update Website

- ☐ Write/Send Press Release
- ☐ Research Email Services
- ☐ Order Promotional Material
- ☐ Contact Advertisers
- ☐ Compose Ad Copy
- ☐ Buy/Create Ad Images
- ☐ Schedule Ads
- ☐ Schedule Social Media Posts
- ☐ Update Backmatter Buy-links
- ☐ Upload Final Files
- ☐ Claim Title: Amazon/Bookbub
- ☐ Release Day Newsletter Push
- ☐ Schedule Reader Contests

© Plot Your Work

Duration to Write:_____ **Release Date:**_____ ☐ **In Production** ☐ **WiP** ☐ **Done**

Progress Meter:
(fill in for each 10% completed)

Third Quarter

week   month 7

1

2

3

4

5

week   month 8

1

2

3

4

5

week   month 9

1

2

3

4

5

Additional Tasks:

☐

☐

☐

☐

☐

☐

☐

☐

☐

☐

☐

☐

☐

☐

☐

☐

Fourth Quarter

week   month 10

1

2

3

4

5

week   month 11

1

2

3

4

5

week   month 12

1

2

3

4

5

Notes

Notes, Marketing Plan, Character Sketches, World Building, Mind Mapping, Bullet Journaling, Doodling, or To-Do Lists:

Notes Area

Title:_____ **Projected MS Length:** _____ **Words Per Day:**_____

Pick a reward (Treat Yo' Self) for completing this project: _____

First Quarter

week		month 1
1		
2		
3		
4		
5		

week		month 2
1		
2		
3		
4		
5		

week		month 3
1		
2		
3		
4		
5		

Second Quarter

week		month 4
1		
2		
3		
4		
5		

week		month 5
1		
2		
3		
4		
5		

week		month 6
1		
2		
3		
4		
5		

The following Sample Tasks are meant to **assist** in filling out a project plan, the suggestions are **not** meant to alter your existing processes**:**

- ☐ Brainstorm
- ☐ Character Sketches
- ☐ Research
- ☐ Begin Plot
- ☐ Finish Plot
- ☐ Compose Full Outline
- ☐ Create Map
- ☐ Create Timeline
- ☐ Set Word Count per day
- ☐ Write First Draft
- ☐ Write Synopsis
- ☐ Self-edit
- ☐ Revise
- ☐ Edit via Program or App

- ☐ Write Book Description
- ☐ Send to Alpha Readers
- ☐ Revise again
- ☐ Send to Editor
- ☐ Incorporate Edits & Revisions
- ☐ Send to Beta Readers
- ☐ Revise/Edit again
- ☐ Submit to Agent
- ☐ Submit to Publisher
- ☐ Send to Proofreader
- ☐ Final Pass Before Format
- ☐ Research Cover Artists
- ☐ Order Cover: **eBook / Print**

- ☐ Finalize Cover
- ☐ Schedule Cover Reveal
- ☐ Format eBook (Self)
- ☐ Send to Formatter
- ☐ Galley Edits
- ☐ Format Print (Self)
- ☐ Inspect Finals
- ☐ Upload Files for Pre-order
- ☐ Contact Reviewers
- ☐ Develop Marketing Plan
- ☐ Sale on Backlist
- ☐ Send Updates to Newsletter
- ☐ Update Website

- ☐ Write/Send Press Release
- ☐ Research Email Services
- ☐ Order Promotional Material
- ☐ Contact Advertisers
- ☐ Compose Ad Copy
- ☐ Buy/Create Ad Images
- ☐ Schedule Ads
- ☐ Schedule Social Media Posts
- ☐ Update Backmatter Buy-links
- ☐ Upload Final Files
- ☐ Claim Title: Amazon/Bookbub
- ☐ Release Day Newsletter Push
- ☐ Schedule Reader Contests

　　　　　© **Plot Your Work**

Duration to Write:_____   **Release Date:**_____   ☐ **In Production**   ☐ **WiP**   ☐ **Done**

Progress Meter:
(fill in for each 10% completed)

Third Quarter

week	month 7
1	
2	
3	
4	
5	

week	month 8
1	
2	
3	
4	
5	

week	month 9
1	
2	
3	
4	
5	

Additional Tasks:

☐   ☐
☐   ☐
☐   ☐
☐   ☐
☐   ☐
☐   ☐
☐   ☐
☐   ☐

Fourth Quarter

week	month 10
1	
2	
3	
4	
5	

week	month 11
1	
2	
3	
4	
5	

week	month 12
1	
2	
3	
4	
5	

Notes

Notes, Marketing Plan, Character Sketches, World Building, Mind Mapping, Bullet Journaling, Doodling, or To-Do Lists:

Yearly Project Planning   **Project Four**

Title:_____ **Projected MS Length:** _____ **Words Per Day:**_____

Pick a reward (Treat Yo' Self) for completing this project: _____

First Quarter

week   month 1

1
....
2
....
3
....
4
....
5
....

week   month 2

1
....
2
....
3
....
4
....
5
....

week   month 3

1
....
2
....
3
....
4
....
5
....

Second Quarter

week   month 4

1
....
2
....
3
....
4
....
5
....

week   month 5

1
....
2
....
3
....
4
....
5
....

week   month 6

1
....
2
....
3
....
4
....
5
....

The following Sample Tasks are meant to **assist** in filling out a project plan, the suggestions are **not** meant to alter your existing processes:

- ☐ Brainstorm
- ☐ Character Sketches
- ☐ Research
- ☐ Begin Plot
- ☐ Finish Plot
- ☐ Compose Full Outline
- ☐ Create Map
- ☐ Create Timeline
- ☐ Set Word Count per day
- ☐ Write First Draft
- ☐ Write Synopsis
- ☐ Self-edit
- ☐ Revise
- ☐ Edit via Program or App

- ☐ Write Book Description
- ☐ Send to Alpha Readers
- ☐ Revise again
- ☐ Send to Editor
- ☐ Incorporate Edits & Revisions
- ☐ Send to Beta Readers
- ☐ Revise/Edit again
- ☐ Submit to Agent
- ☐ Submit to Publisher
- ☐ Send to Proofreader
- ☐ Final Pass Before Format
- ☐ Research Cover Artists
- ☐ Order Cover: **eBook / Print**

- ☐ Finalize Cover
- ☐ Schedule Cover Reveal
- ☐ Format eBook (Self)
- ☐ Send to Formatter
- ☐ Galley Edits
- ☐ Format Print (Self)
- ☐ Inspect Finals
- ☐ Upload Files for Pre-order
- ☐ Contact Reviewers
- ☐ Develop Marketing Plan
- ☐ Sale on Backlist
- ☐ Send Updates to Newsletter
- ☐ Update Website

- ☐ Write/Send Press Release
- ☐ Research Email Services
- ☐ Order Promotional Material
- ☐ Contact Advertisers
- ☐ Compose Ad Copy
- ☐ Buy/Create Ad Images
- ☐ Schedule Ads
- ☐ Schedule Social Media Posts
- ☐ Update Backmatter Buy-links
- ☐ Upload Final Files
- ☐ Claim Title: Amazon/Bookbub
- ☐ Release Day Newsletter Push
- ☐ Schedule Reader Contests

© **Plot Your Work**

Duration to Write:_____ **Release Date:**_____ ☐ **In Production** ☐ **WiP** ☐ **Done**

Progress Meter:
(fill in for each 10% completed)

Third Quarter

week	month 7
1	
2	
3	
4	
5	

week	month 8
1	
2	
3	
4	
5	

week	month 9
1	
2	
3	
4	
5	

Additional Tasks:

☐
☐
☐
☐
☐
☐
☐

☐
☐
☐
☐
☐
☐
☐

Fourth Quarter

week	month 10
1	
2	
3	
4	
5	

week	month 11
1	
2	
3	
4	
5	

week	month 12
1	
2	
3	
4	
5	

Notes

Notes, Marketing Plan, Character Sketches, World Building, Mind Mapping, Bullet Journaling, Doodling, or To-Do Lists:

Title:_____ **Projected MS Length:** _____ **Words Per Day:**_____

Pick a reward (Treat Yo' Self) for completing this project: _____

First Quarter

week　　　　　　　　　　　　　　　　　　　month 1

1
....
2
....
3
....
4
....
5
....

....

week　　　　　　　　　　　　　　　　　　　month 2

1
....
2
....
3
....
4
....
5
....

....

week　　　　　　　　　　　　　　　　　　　month 3

1
....
2
....
3
....
4
....
5
....

....

Second Quarter

week　　　　　　　　　　　　　　　　　　　month 4

1
....
2
....
3
....
4
....
5
....

....

week　　　　　　　　　　　　　　　　　　　month 5

1
....
2
....
3
....
4
....
5
....

....

week　　　　　　　　　　　　　　　　　　　month 6

1
....
2
....
3
....
4
....
5
....

....

The following Sample Tasks are meant to **assist** in filling out a project plan, the suggestions are **not** meant to alter your existing processes:

- ☐ Brainstorm
- ☐ Character Sketches
- ☐ Research
- ☐ Begin Plot
- ☐ Finish Plot
- ☐ Compose Full Outline
- ☐ Create Map
- ☐ Create Timeline
- ☐ Set Word Count per day
- ☐ Write First Draft
- ☐ Write Synopsis
- ☐ Self-edit
- ☐ Revise
- ☐ Edit via Program or App

- ☐ Write Book Description
- ☐ Send to Alpha Readers
- ☐ Revise again
- ☐ Send to Editor
- ☐ Incorporate Edits & Revisions
- ☐ Send to Beta Readers
- ☐ Revise/Edit again
- ☐ Submit to Agent
- ☐ Submit to Publisher
- ☐ Send to Proofreader
- ☐ Final Pass Before Format
- ☐ Research Cover Artists
- ☐ Order Cover: **eBook / Print**

- ☐ Finalize Cover
- ☐ Schedule Cover Reveal
- ☐ Format eBook (Self)
- ☐ Send to Formatter
- ☐ Galley Edits
- ☐ Format Print (Self)
- ☐ Inspect Finals
- ☐ Upload Files for Pre-order
- ☐ Contact Reviewers
- ☐ Develop Marketing Plan
- ☐ Sale on Backlist
- ☐ Send Updates to Newsletter
- ☐ Update Website

- ☐ Write/Send Press Release
- ☐ Research Email Services
- ☐ Order Promotional Material
- ☐ Contact Advertisers
- ☐ Compose Ad Copy
- ☐ Buy/Create Ad Images
- ☐ Schedule Ads
- ☐ Schedule Social Media Posts
- ☐ Update Backmatter Buy-links
- ☐ Upload Final Files
- ☐ Claim Title: Amazon/Bookbub
- ☐ Release Day Newsletter Push
- ☐ Schedule Reader Contests

Duration to Write:_____　**Release Date:**_____　☐ **In Production**　☐ **WiP**　☐ **Done**

Progress Meter:
(fill in for each 10% completed)

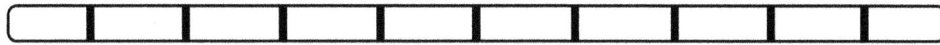

Third Quarter

week	month 7
1	
2	
3	
4	
5	

week	month 8
1	
2	
3	
4	
5	

week	month 9
1	
2	
3	
4	
5	

Additional Tasks:

☐
☐
☐
☐
☐
☐
☐

☐
☐
☐
☐
☐
☐
☐

Fourth Quarter

week	month 10
1	
2	
3	
4	
5	

week	month 11
1	
2	
3	
4	
5	

week	month 12
1	
2	
3	
4	
5	

Notes

© Plot Your Work

Notes, Marketing Plan, Character Sketches, World Building, Mind Mapping, Bullet Journaling, Doodling, or To-Do Lists:

Three Month Goal Planner
Look back over the first three months from each project plan. Transfer tasks into concrete goals. Check off when complete. Try not to over-commit on your first quarter.

Goal:	Goal:	Goal:
Project:	**Project:**	**Project:**
Due Date:	**Due Date:**	**Due Date:**
Tasks to complete this Goal:	**Tasks to complete this Goal:**	**Tasks to complete this Goal:**
☐ 1	☐ 1	☐ 1
☐ 2	☐ 2	☐ 2
☐ 3	☐ 3	☐ 3
☐ 4	☐ 4	☐ 4
☐ 5	☐ 5	☐ 5
☐ 6	☐ 6	☐ 6
☐ 7	☐ 7	☐ 7

Goal:	Goal:	Goal:
Project:	**Project:**	**Project:**
Due Date:	**Due Date:**	**Due Date:**
Tasks to complete this Goal:	**Tasks to complete this Goal:**	**Tasks to complete this Goal:**
☐ 1	☐ 1	☐ 1
☐ 2	☐ 2	☐ 2
☐ 3	☐ 3	☐ 3
☐ 4	☐ 4	☐ 4
☐ 5	☐ 5	☐ 5
☐ 6	☐ 6	☐ 6
☐ 7	☐ 7	☐ 7

Goal:	Goal:	Goal:
Project:	**Project:**	**Project:**
Due Date:	**Due Date:**	**Due Date:**
Tasks to complete this Goal:	**Tasks to complete this Goal:**	**Tasks to complete this Goal:**
☐ 1	☐ 1	☐ 1
☐ 2	☐ 2	☐ 2
☐ 3	☐ 3	☐ 3
☐ 4	☐ 4	☐ 4
☐ 5	☐ 5	☐ 5
☐ 6	☐ 6	☐ 6
☐ 7	☐ 7	☐ 7

First 30 Days

Look over tasks from the Three Month Planner and list below one to two from each project. Do not over-plan during this first month. Adjust to these new organizational methods and stay on track. Completing eight to ten is much better than quitting halfway because you're overwhelmed.

Quarterly Goal Focus Items for Next 30 Days:

☐ ☐ ☐ ☐ ☐

☐ ☐ ☐ ☐ ☐

☐ ☐ ☐ ☐ ☐

☐ ☐ ☐ ☐ ☐

Circle the box for the three tasks that need to be done first. Move those to your first weekly action plan.

*Each week you'll review this page, check off completed tasks, circle next items, and then move them to the next weekly action plan.

Look at the items above. Do any need to be broken down further? Do you know how to handle each? Do any require outside help? Use the space below, if needed, to expand on what each task will require for you to succeed in completing it.

Monthly Planner for:_____ (which Social Media account)   Day(s) to Schedule:_____

What to post and when. Schedule ahead! Check project calendars first, then add the relevant post info below. Fill in the rest with targeted audience content, things that make you laugh, or share posts from your newsfeed that caught your attention and you think your readers might enjoy.   *Check next to day when you've scheduled the post

—> Interior columns can be used for multiple accounts, multiple posts, or ignored. Use only if needed.<—

Date	Type of Post(s)	Time	PtP
☐			
☐			
☐			
☐			
☐			
☐			
☐			
☐			
☐			
☐			
☐			
☐			
☐			
☐			
☐			
☐			
☐			
☐			
☐			
☐			
☐			
☐			
☐			
☐			
☐			
☐			
☐			
☐			
☐			
☐			
☐			

PtP = Paid to Promote

Go back and review the stats from your account. Which type of content performed the best? Highlight the top ten **non-paid** posts from the past month. Moving forward, create similar content, or expand on the theme to better reach your audience. Which posts did you **P**ay to **P**romote? Want to track the stats? Create a hand-made table on a dot-grid page of your choosing. You can do this!

         © **Plot Your Work**

Week One: _____/_____/_____

Top Three Focus Items from Monthly Breakdown: Are you feeling strong? Attempt a bonus task:

☐   ☐   ☐   ☐

Weekly Action Plan: *Add to your regular weekly planner/agenda. Besides your daily writing time, what else do you need to accomplish? Admin work, cover design, editing, research? Block time for focus items first, then be realistic with what you can handle.

Date

: ☐

: ☐

: ☐

: ☐

: ☐

: ☐

: ☐

Week in Review: Did you finish all the tasks? Circle which ones need to move to next week and carve time out of your schedule to do them in addition to the ones you'll have for the upcoming week. The only way to succeed is to stick to a plan and keep at it, even when you have setbacks, sick days, and personal issues. Don't give up.

Regroup and keep going.

Week Two: _____/_____/_____

Next Three Focus Items from Monthly Breakdown: Are you feeling strong? Attempt a bonus task:

☐   ☐   ☐   ☐

Weekly Action Plan: *Add to your regular weekly planner/agenda. Block time for focus items first, then be realistic with what else you can handle daily. Check your regular agenda and remember to schedule time for **you.**

"To gain your own voice, you have to forget about having it heard." —Allen Ginsberg

Date

: ☐

: ☐

: ☐

: ☐

: ☐

: ☐

: ☐

Week in Review: Read previous week's prompt and get to it!

Week Three: ____/____/____

Next Three Focus Items from Monthly Breakdown: Are you feeling strong? Attempt a bonus task:

☐   ☐   ☐   ☐

Weekly Action Plan: *Add to your regular weekly planner/agenda.

"Literature is strewn with the wreckage of men who have minded beyond reason the opinions of others." —Virginia Woolf

Date

    :   ☐

    :   ☐

    :   ☐

    :   ☐

    :   ☐

    :   ☐

    :   ☐

Week in Review: Every week you need to do the same thing — review what you accomplished and plan which tasks to do next week.

Week Four: ____/____/____

Next Three Focus Items from Monthly Breakdown: Are you feeling strong? Attempt a bonus task:

☐   ☐   ☐   ☐

Weekly Action Plan: *Add to your regular weekly planner/agenda.

"It's not that I'm so smart, it's just that I stay with problems longer." —Albert Einstein

Date

    :   ☐

    :   ☐

    :   ☐

    :   ☐

    :   ☐

    :   ☐

    :   ☐

Week in Review: Check off what you did, circle and move what you didn't, and plan next week's tasks. You got this.

Days 29-31 (as needed): _____/_____/_____

Last Focus Items from Monthly Breakdown:

☐   ☐   ☐   ☐

Weekly Action Plan: *Map out what needs to be done when and add to your regular weekly planner/agenda

"Write. Rewrite. When not writing or rewriting, read. I know of no shortcuts." —Larry L. King

Date

:   ☐

:   ☐

:   ☐

:   ☐

:   ☐

Month in Review: Be honest. Overcommitting only perpetuates feelings of failure and inadequacy. Who the hell needs that? Did your plans fall apart or were you able to stay on task and complete what was needed? A plan is only as good as its end user: **YOU.**

The goal in using this planner is to succeed in all your projects, not to make yourself feel bad or so overwhelmed you run screaming from the house. If everything you wanted to accomplish didn't happen, learn from it. Alter your habits moving forward. Adjust your expectations. Or give yourself the kick in the ass you need to finally **actualize** your dreams. It's your choice. It always has been.

Newsletter: When was your newsletter sent?: _____ Day and Time: _____ Day One Open Rate: _____ Day Five, Total Open Rate:_____ High Spam report? If yes, why? Fix it next month to lower spam ratings. Did you cross-post your newsletter to social media? Consider paying to promote the post to your existing followers. Your newsletter is only a valuable marketing tool if people READ IT. Dynamic subject lines, split testing on subject lines, day and time of the week you send—they all matter. Track what you're doing and refine your process. What can you do next month to increase your reach?

Social Media: Total # of Scheduled Posts: _____ Total # of Live Posts: _____ Total Reach for Month: _____ What type of posts had the most views? The most likes and comments? Go back and highlight them in your Social Media Planning section for this month. What days each week will you create content for next month? _____ What day next month will you schedule your content? _____ **Make a note of the days on your regular agenda. **Stick to the plan.**

Website Data: What are you tracking and why? Do you need to create a table in your next monthly dot-grid section for tracking analytics better? Then DO IT. See what needs to be done and take action. Don't expect any planner to take the real work out of tracking exactly what **you** need.

Second 30 Days

Look over tasks from your Three Month Planner and list below two to five from each project. Decide how much you can handle based on last month's review. Over-scheduling your day leads to failure of some kind, even if the failure is time spent on you, your health, or your family. **Find Your Balance.** Don't give up.

Quarterly Goal Focus Items for Next 30 Days:

☐   ☐   ☐   ☐   ☐

☐   ☐   ☐   ☐   ☐

☐   ☐   ☐   ☐   ☐

☐   ☐   ☐   ☐   ☐

☐   ☐   ☐   ☐   ☐

Circle the box for the three to four tasks that need to be done first .Move those to your first weekly action plan.

*Each week you'll review this page, check off completed tasks, circle next items, and then move them to the next weekly action plan.

Look at the items above. Do any need to be broken down further? Do you know how to handle each? Do any require outside help? Use the space below, if needed, to expand on what each task will require for you to succeed in completing it.

Monthly Planner for:_____ (which Social Media account)   Day(s) to Schedule:_____

What to post and when. Schedule ahead! Check project calendars first, then add the relevant post info below. Fill in the rest with targeted audience content, things that make you laugh, or share posts from your newsfeed that caught your attention and you think your readers might enjoy.   *Check next to day when you've scheduled the post

—> Interior columns can be used for multiple accounts, multiple posts, or ignored. Use only if needed.<—

Date	Type of Post(s)			Time	PtP
☐					
☐					
☐					
☐					
☐					
☐					
☐					
☐					
☐					
☐					
☐					
☐					
☐					
☐					
☐					
☐					
☐					
☐					
☐					
☐					
☐					
☐					
☐					
☐					
☐					
☐					
☐					
☐					
☐					

PtP = Paid to Promote

Go back and review the stats from your account. Which type of content performed the best? Highlight the top ten **non-paid** posts from the past month. Moving forward, create similar content, or expand on the theme to better reach your audience. Which posts did you **P**ay **to P**romote? Want to track the stats? Create a hand-made table on a dot-grid page of your choosing. You can do this!

Week One: _____/_____/_____

Top Three Focus Items from Monthly Breakdown:

Are you feeling strong? Attempt a bonus task:

☐   ☐   ☐   ☐

Weekly Action Plan: *Add to your regular weekly planner/agenda. Besides your daily writing time, what else do you need to accomplish? Admin work, cover design, editing, research? Block time for focus items first, then be realistic with what you can handle.

"We are all apprentices in a craft where no one ever becomes a master." —Ernest Hemingway

Date

_____ : _____   ☐

_____ : _____   ☐

_____ : _____   ☐

_____ : _____   ☐

_____ : _____   ☐

_____ : _____   ☐

_____ : _____   ☐

Week in Review: How is the plan coming along? Everything running smoothly? The hard part comes from you, not this planner. Do. The. Work. There is no other way.

Week Two: _____/_____/_____

Next Three Focus Items from Monthly Breakdown:

Are you feeling strong? Attempt a bonus task:

☐   ☐   ☐   ☐

Weekly Action Plan: Map out what needs to be done and DO IT. Check your regular agenda and remember to schedule time for **you.**

"I do not over-intellectualize the production process. I try to keep it simple: Tell the damned story." —Tom Clancy

Date

_____ : _____   ☐

_____ : _____   ☐

_____ : _____   ☐

_____ : _____   ☐

_____ : _____   ☐

_____ : _____   ☐

_____ : _____   ☐

Week in Review: Check off tasks, move incomplete ones to next week. Get it done!

Week Three: _____/_____/_____

Next Three Focus Items from Monthly Breakdown: Are you feeling strong? Attempt a bonus task:

☐   ☐   ☐   ☐

Weekly Action Plan: *Add to your regular weekly planner/agenda.

"I always start writing with a clean piece of paper and a dirty mind." —Patrick Dennis

Date

_____ : _____ ☐

_____ : _____ ☐

_____ : _____ ☐

_____ : _____ ☐

_____ : _____ ☐

_____ : _____ ☐

_____ : _____ ☐

Week in Review: Circle unfinished tasks and move to next week. Make time to complete them in addition to the ones you'll have for the upcoming week.

Week Four: _____/_____/_____

Next Three Focus Items from Monthly Breakdown: Are you feeling strong? Attempt a bonus task:

☐   ☐   ☐   ☐

Weekly Action Plan: *Add to your regular weekly planner/agenda.

"Let me tell you the secret that has led to my goal. My strength lies solely in my tenacity." —Louis Pasteur

Date

_____ : _____ ☐

_____ : _____ ☐

_____ : _____ ☐

_____ : _____ ☐

_____ : _____ ☐

_____ : _____ ☐

_____ : _____ ☐

Week in Review: Check off what you did, circle and move what you didn't, and plan next week's tasks. You got this.

Days 29-31 (as needed): _____/_____/_____

Last Focus Items from Monthly Breakdown:

☐　　　　　　　☐　　　　　　　☐　　　　☐

Weekly Action Plan: *Map out what needs to be done when and add the tasks to your regular weekly planner/agenda

"The difference between the almost right word and the right word is... the difference between the lightning bug and the lightning." —Mark Twain

Date

: _____ ☐

: _____ ☐

: _____ ☐

: _____ ☐

: _____ ☐

Month in Review: Are you consistently meeting your tasks each week? Amp things up in your next month. **Are you falling behind and getting stressed?** Map out a new plan. Try, try again. Never quit!

What can you do to help yourself succeed? Get up early, hire help, or outline better so your writing time is more fruitful. Excuses will get you the same results you had in the past, and isn't the point to improve as we move forward?

Newsletter: Date of last newsletter? Day and Time: _____ Day One Open Rate: _____ Day Five, Total Open Rate:_____ High Spam report? If yes, why? Fix it next month to lower spam ratings. What can you do next month to increase your reach? Ideas for writing may come to us at any time, but often marketing and promotion isn't second nature. Read, research, learn — you wrote a book, you can do ANYTHING. Ideas on increasing your open rate:

_____

_____

_____

Social Media: Total # of Scheduled Posts: _____ Total # of Live Posts: _____ Total Reach for Month: _____
What type of posts had the most views? The most likes and comments? Go back and highlight them in your Social Media Planning section for this month. What days each week will you create content for next month? _____ What day next month will you schedule your content? _____ **Make a note of the days on your regular agenda. **Stick to the plan.**

_____

_____

_____

Website Data: Have you checked out the websites from other authors in your genre who are doing well? What's the first thing you see on their site? How prominent is their newsletter signup form? If a reader searched for you on the Internet and found your website, how could you entice them to sign up for your newsletter?

_____

_____

　　　　　　　　　　　　　　　　　　　　　　© **Plot Your Work**

Third 30 Days

Look over tasks from your Three Month Goals and list below three to six from each project. Adjusting to new organizational habits can take time. Don't give up. Completing ten to twelve is much better than accomplishing nothing. Never stop trying.

Quarterly Goal Focus Items for Next 30 Days:

☐　　　☐　　　☐　　　☐　　　☐

☐　　　☐　　　☐　　　☐　　　☐

☐　　　☐　　　☐　　　☐　　　☐

☐　　　☐　　　☐　　　☐　　　☐

☐　　　☐　　　☐　　　☐　　　☐

Circle the box for the four tasks that need to be done first. Move those to your first weekly action plan.

*Each week you'll review this page, check off completed tasks, circle next items, and then move them to the next weekly action plan.

Look at the items above. Do any need to be broken down further? Do you know how to handle each? Do any require outside help? Use the space below, if needed, to expand on what each task will require for you to succeed in completing it.

Monthly Planner for:_____ (which Social Media account)   Day(s) to Schedule:_____

What to post and when. Schedule ahead! Check project calendars first, then add the relevant post info below. Fill in the rest with targeted audience content, things that make you laugh, or share posts from your newsfeed that caught your attention and you think your readers might enjoy.   *Check next to day when you've scheduled the post

—> Interior columns can be used for multiple accounts, multiple posts, or ignored. Use only if needed.<—

Date	Type of Post(s)	Time	PtP
☐			
☐			
☐			
☐			
☐			
☐			
☐			
☐			
☐			
☐			
☐			
☐			
☐			
☐			
☐			
☐			
☐			
☐			
☐			
☐			
☐			
☐			
☐			
☐			
☐			
☐			
☐			
☐			
☐			
☐			
☐			

PtP = Paid to Promote

Go back and review the stats from your account. Which type of content performed the best? Highlight the top ten **non-paid** posts from the past month. Moving forward, create similar content, or expand on the theme to better reach your audience. Which posts did you **P**ay **t**o **P**romote? Want to track the stats? Create a hand-made table on a dot-grid page of your choosing. You can do this!

Week One: _____/_____/_____

Top Three Focus Items from Monthly Breakdown:　　　　　Are you feeling strong? Attempt a bonus task:

☐　　　　　　　　☐　　　　　　　　☐　　　　　　　　☐

Weekly Action Plan: Besides your daily writing time, what else do you need to accomplish? Admin work, cover design, editing, research? Block time for focus items first, then be realistic with what you can handle daily.

Date

_____ : _____ ☐

_____ : _____ ☐

_____ : _____ ☐

_____ : _____ ☐

_____ : _____ ☐

_____ : _____ ☐

_____ : _____ ☐

<u>**Week in Review:**</u> Did you finish all the tasks? Circle which ones need to move to next week and carve time out of your schedule to do them in addition to the ones you'll have for the upcoming week. **Regroup and keep going.**

Week Two: _____/_____/_____

Next Three Focus Items from Monthly Breakdown:　　　　　Are you feeling strong? Attempt a bonus task:

☐　　　　　　　　☐　　　　　　　　☐　　　　　　　　☐

Weekly Action Plan: *Map out what needs to be done and add to your regular weekly planner/agenda. Block time for focus items first, then be realistic with what else you can handle daily. Check your regular agenda and remember to schedule time for **you.**

*"I like the process of pencil and paper as opposed to a machine.
I think the writing is better when it's done in handwriting." —Nelson DeMille*

Date

_____ : _____ ☐

_____ : _____ ☐

_____ : _____ ☐

_____ : _____ ☐

_____ : _____ ☐

_____ : _____ ☐

_____ : _____ ☐

<u>**Week in Review:**</u> Read previous week's prompt and get to it!

Week Three: _____/_____/_____

Next Three Focus Items from Monthly Breakdown:

Are you feeling strong? Attempt a bonus task:

☐   ☐   ☐   ☐

Weekly Action Plan: *Add to your regular weekly planner/agenda.

"Failure is only the opportunity to begin again, this time more intelligently." —Henry Ford

Date

    :   ☐

    :   ☐

    :   ☐

    :   ☐

    :   ☐

    :   ☐

    :   ☐

Week in Review: You know the drill by now — hop to it! Why are we writing all this down rather than using an electronic system? The physical act of writing does something in our brain. Makes it real. Makes it solid. Engraves it somehow into our psyche. Don't overanalyze it. Accept it. And write things down.

Week Four: _____/_____/_____

Next Three Focus Items from Monthly Breakdown:

Are you feeling strong? Attempt a bonus task:

☐   ☐   ☐   ☐

Weekly Action Plan: *Add to your regular weekly planner/agenda.

"Either write something worth reading or do something worth writing." —Benjamin Franklin

Date

    :   ☐

    :   ☐

    :   ☐

    :   ☐

    :   ☐

    :   ☐

    :   ☐

Week in Review: Check off what you did, circle and move what you didn't, and plan next week's tasks. You got this.

Days 29-31 (as needed): _____ / _____ / _____

Last Focus Items from Monthly Breakdown:

☐	☐	☐	☐

Weekly Action Plan: *Map out what needs to be done when and add to your regular weekly planner/agenda

> *"Artists don't talk about art. Artists talk about work. If I have anything to say to young writers, it's stop thinking of writing as art. Think of it as work."* —Paddy Chayefsky

Date

_____ : _____ ☐

_____ : _____ ☐

_____ : _____ ☐

_____ : _____ ☐

_____ : _____ ☐

Quarterly Review:

What worked? Did you see an improvement to your organizational efforts? What changes do you need to make moving forward to meet your goals and dreams? How do you need to alter your day to do more? Use the area below to tweak your efforts, makes lists, or track what was achieved.

_____

_____

_____

_____

_____

_____

_____

_____

_____

_____

_____

_____

　　　　　　　　　　　　　　　　　　　　　　© Plot Your Work

Second Quarter   Months: _____ to _____

Three Month Goal Planner
Look back over the second three months from each project plan. Transfer tasks into concrete goals. Check off when complete.

Goal:

Project:

Due Date:

Tasks to complete this Goal:

□ 1

□ 2

□ 3

□ 4

□ 5

□ 6

□ 7

Goal:

Project:

Due Date:

Tasks to complete this Goal:

□ 1

□ 2

□ 3

□ 4

□ 5

□ 6

□ 7

Goal:

Project:

Due Date:

Tasks to complete this Goal:

□ 1

□ 2

□ 3

□ 4

□ 5

□ 6

□ 7

Goal:

Project:

Due Date:

Tasks to complete this Goal:

□ 1

□ 2

□ 3

□ 4

□ 5

□ 6

□ 7

Goal:

Project:

Due Date:

Tasks to complete this Goal:

□ 1

□ 2

□ 3

□ 4

□ 5

□ 6

□ 7

Goal:

Project:

Due Date:

Tasks to complete this Goal:

□ 1

□ 2

□ 3

□ 4

□ 5

□ 6

□ 7

Goal:

Project:

Due Date:

Tasks to complete this Goal:

□ 1

□ 2

□ 3

□ 4

□ 5

□ 6

□ 7

Goal:

Project:

Due Date:

Tasks to complete this Goal:

□ 1

□ 2

□ 3

□ 4

□ 5

□ 6

□ 7

Goal:

Project:

Due Date:

Tasks to complete this Goal:

□ 1

□ 2

□ 3

□ 4

□ 5

□ 6

□ 7

© Plot Your Work

First 30 Days

Look over tasks from the Three Month Goal Planner and list below three to five from each project. If you've stayed on track—great work! If not, what the hell are you waiting for? We may have designed the sheets, but you laid out the work you could handle. Get your head clear and your mind focused. You Can Do This.

Quarterly Goal Focus Items for Next 30 Days:

☐   ☐   ☐   ☐   ☐

☐   ☐   ☐   ☐   ☐

☐   ☐   ☐   ☐   ☐

☐   ☐   ☐   ☐   ☐

☐   ☐   ☐   ☐   ☐

Circle the box for the three tasks that need to be done first. Move those to your first weekly action plan.

*Each week you'll review this page, check off completed tasks, circle next items, and then move them to the next weekly action plan.

Look at the items above. Do any need to be broken down further? Do you know how to handle each? Do any require outside help? Use the space below, if needed, to expand on what each task will require for you to succeed in completing it.

Monthly Planner for:_____ (which Social Media account)   Day(s) to Schedule:_____

What to post and when. Schedule ahead! Check project calendars first, then add the relevant post info below. Fill in the rest with targeted audience content, things that make you laugh, or share posts from your newsfeed that caught your attention and you think your readers might enjoy.   *Check next to day when you've scheduled the post

—> Interior columns can be used for multiple accounts, multiple posts, or ignored. Use only if needed.<—

Date	Type of Post(s)			Time	PtP
☐					
☐					
☐					
☐					
☐					
☐					
☐					
☐					
☐					
☐					
☐					
☐					
☐					
☐					
☐					
☐					
☐					
☐					
☐					
☐					
☐					
☐					
☐					
☐					
☐					
☐					
☐					
☐					
☐					
☐					
☐					

PtP = Paid to Promote

Go back and review the stats from your account. Which type of content performed the best? Highlight the top ten **non-paid** posts from the past month. Moving forward, create similar content, or expand on the theme to better reach your audience. Which posts did you **P**ay **to P**romote? Want to track the stats? Create a hand-made table on a dot-grid page of your choosing. You can do this!

© **Plot Your Work**

Week One: _____ / _____ / _____

Top Three Focus Items from Monthly Breakdown:

Are you feeling strong? Attempt a bonus task:

☐   ☐   ☐   ☐

Weekly Action Plan: No matter how much you wish or how much you plan, the simple truth is shit won't get done unless you do it.

"Success is the sum of small efforts, repeated day in and day out." —Robert Collier

Date

_____ : _____ ☐

_____ : _____ ☐

_____ : _____ ☐

_____ : _____ ☐

_____ : _____ ☐

_____ : _____ ☐

_____ : _____ ☐

Week in Review: Month four! Don't give up now. **Regroup and keep going.**

Week Two: _____ / _____ / _____

Next Three Focus Items from Monthly Breakdown:

Are you feeling strong? Attempt a bonus task:

☐   ☐   ☐   ☐

Weekly Action Plan: *Add to your regular weekly planner/agenda. Block time for focus items first, then be realistic with what else you can handle daily. Check your regular agenda and remember to schedule time for **you.**

"The road to hell is paved with works-in-progress." —Philip Roth

Date

_____ : _____ ☐

_____ : _____ ☐

_____ : _____ ☐

_____ : _____ ☐

_____ : _____ ☐

_____ : _____ ☐

_____ : _____ ☐

Week in Review: Read previous week's prompt and get to it!

Week Three: ____/____/____

Next Three Focus Items from Monthly Breakdown:

Are you feeling strong? Attempt a bonus task:

☐   ☐   ☐   ☐

Weekly Action Plan: *Add to your regular weekly planner/agenda.
"I don't care if a reader hates one of my stories, just as long as he finishes the book." —Roald Dahl

Date

       : .... ☐

       : .... ☐

       : .... ☐

       : .... ☐

       : .... ☐

       : .... ☐

       : .... ☐

Week in Review: Every week you need to do the same thing — review what you accomplished and plan which tasks to do next week.

Week Four: ____/____/____

Next Three Focus Items from Monthly Breakdown:

Are you feeling strong? Attempt a bonus task:

☐   ☐   ☐   ☐

Weekly Action Plan: *Add to your regular weekly planner/agenda.
"It's none of their business that you have to learn to write. Let them think you were born that way." —Ernest Hemingway

Date

       : .... ☐

       : .... ☐

       : .... ☐

       : .... ☐

       : .... ☐

       : .... ☐

       : .... ☐

Week in Review: Check off what you did, circle and move what you didn't, and plan next week's tasks. You got this.

Days 29-31 (as needed): _____ / _____ / _____

Last Focus Items from Monthly Breakdown:

☐   ☐   ☐   ☐

Weekly Action Plan: *Map out what needs to be done when and add to your regular weekly planner/agenda

"Every secret of a writer's soul, every experience of his life, every quality of his mind, is written large in his works."—Virginia Woolf

Date

.... : .... ☐

.... : .... ☐

.... : .... ☐

.... : .... ☐

.... : .... ☐

.... : .... ☐

Month in Review: If everything you wanted to accomplish didn't happen, learn from it. Alter your habits moving forward. Adjust your expectations. You're not ready to give up, are you? Good! Because quitters don't publish, they just talk a lot of crap at parties and make you want to punch them.

Newsletter: When was your newsletter sent?: Day and Time: _____ Day One Open Rate: _____ Day Five, Total Open Rate:_____ Has anything happened to you recently, have you gone anywhere interesting, or have you learned something cool that your readers might want to hear about? Make note of it here and include it in your next newsletter:

....

....

....

Social Media: Total # of Scheduled Posts: _____ Total # of Live Posts: _____ Total Reach for Month: _____ What type of posts had the most views? The most likes and comments? Go back and highlight them in your Social Media Planning section for this month. What days each week will you create content for next month? _____ What day next month will you schedule your content? _____ **Make a note of the days on your regular agenda. Stick to the plan.**

....

....

....

Website Data: Have you had a new title release? Did you include your latest newsletter on your website? Did you create any new content worth sharing? Make note of it here and update your website. Or, if you'd rather list stats, go for it. It's your planner, use it how you need it!

....

....

Second 30 Days

Look over tasks from your Three Month Planner and list below three to five from each project. Decide how much you can handle based on last month's review. Over-scheduling your day leads to failure of some kind, even if the failure is time spent on you, your health, or your family. **Find Your Balance.** Don't give up.

Quarterly Goal Focus Items for Next 30 Days:

☐   ☐   ☐   ☐   ☐

☐   ☐   ☐   ☐   ☐

☐   ☐   ☐   ☐   ☐

☐   ☐   ☐   ☐   ☐

☐   ☐   ☐   ☐   ☐

Circle the box for the three tasks that need to be done first. Move those to your first weekly action plan.

*Each week you'll review this page, check off completed tasks, circle next items, and then move them to the next weekly action plan.

Look at the items above. Do any need to be broken down further? Do you know how to handle each? Do any require outside help? Use the space below, if needed, to expand on what each task will require for you to succeed in completing it.

© **Plot Your Work**

Monthly Planner for:_____ (which Social Media account)   Day(s) to Schedule:_____

What to post, and when. Schedule ahead! Check project calendars first, then add the relevant post info below. Fill in the rest with targeted audience content, things that make you laugh, or share posts from your newsfeed that caught your attention and you think your readers might enjoy.   *Check next to day when you've scheduled the post

—> Interior columns can be used for multiple accounts, multiple posts, or ignored. Use only if needed.<—

Date	Type of Post(s)			Time	PtP
☐					
☐					
☐					
☐					
☐					
☐					
☐					
☐					
☐					
☐					
☐					
☐					
☐					
☐					
☐					
☐					
☐					
☐					
☐					
☐					
☐					
☐					
☐					
☐					
☐					
☐					
☐					
☐					
☐					
☐					
☐					

PtP = Paid to Promote

Go back and review the stats from your account. Which type of content performed the best? Highlight the top ten **non-paid** posts from the past month. Moving forward, create similar content, or expand on the theme to better reach your audience. Which posts did you **P**ay **t**o **P**romote? Want to track the stats? Create a hand-made table on a dot-grid page of your choosing. You can do this!

Week One: _____ / _____ / _____

Top Three Focus Items from Monthly Breakdown: Are you feeling strong? Attempt a bonus task:

☐   ☐   ☐   ☐

Weekly Action Plan: Besides your daily writing time, what else do you need to accomplish? Admin work, cover design, editing, research? Block time for focus items first, then be realistic with what you can handle daily. Check your regular agenda and remember to schedule time for **you**.

"For your born writer, nothing is so healing as the realization that he has come upon the right word." —Catherine Drinker Bowen

Date

:   ☐

:   ☐

:   ☐

:   ☐

:   ☐

:   ☐

:   ☐

Week in Review: Pat yourself on the back for what you accomplished, reschedule what you didn't, and move forward!

Week Two: _____ / _____ / _____

Next Three Focus Items from Monthly Breakdown: Are you feeling strong? Attempt a bonus task:

☐   ☐   ☐   ☐

Weekly Action Plan: *Add tasks your regular weekly planner/agenda. Don't overcommit.

"The greatest part of a writer's time is spent in reading, in order to write; a man will turn over half a library to make one book." —Samuel Johnson

Date

:   ☐

:   ☐

:   ☐

:   ☐

:   ☐

:   ☐

:   ☐

Week in Review: Read previous week's prompt and get to it!

Week Three: _____/_____/_____
Next Three Focus Items from Monthly Breakdown: Are you feeling strong? Attempt a bonus task:

☐   ☐   ☐   ☐

Weekly Action Plan: *Add to your regular weekly planner/agenda.
"I almost always urge people to write in the first person. ... Writing is an act of ego and you might as well admit it."—William Zinsser

Date
:   ☐
:   ☐
:   ☐
:   ☐
:   ☐
:   ☐
:   ☐

Week in Review: You know the drill — hop to it! You can do this. The trick is to never give up.

Week Four: _____/_____/_____
Next Three Focus Items from Monthly Breakdown: Are you feeling strong? Attempt a bonus task:

☐   ☐   ☐   ☐

Weekly Action Plan: *Add to your regular weekly planner/agenda.
"It took me fifteen years to discover I had no talent for writing, but I couldn't give it up because by that time I was too famous." —Robert Benchley

Date
:   ☐
:   ☐
:   ☐
:   ☐
:   ☐
:   ☐
:   ☐

Week in Review: Check off what you did, circle and move what you didn't, and plan next week's tasks. You got this.

© **Plot Your Work**

Days 29-31 (as needed): _____/_____/_____

Last Focus Items from Monthly Breakdown:

☐   ☐   ☐   ☐

Weekly Action Plan: *Map out what needs to be done when and add to your regular weekly planner/agenda

"If you can't fly then run, if you can't run then walk, if you can't walk then crawl, but whatever you do you have to keep moving forward." —Martin Luther King, Jr.

Date

____ :

☐

____ :

☐

____ :

☐

____ :

☐

____ :

☐

Month in Review: If everything you wanted to accomplish didn't happen, learn from it. Alter your habits moving forward. Adjust your expectations. You're not ready to give up, are you? Good! Because quitters don't publish, they just talk a lot of crap at parties and make you want to punch them.

Newsletter: When was your newsletter sent?: Day and Time: _____ Day One Open Rate: _____ Day Five, Total Open Rate:_____ Use the area below to make notes on what to include in your next newsletter:

Social Media: Total # of Scheduled Posts: _____ Total # of Live Posts: _____ Total Reach for Month: _____ What type of posts had the most views? The most likes and comments? Go back and highlight them in your Social Media Planning section for this month. What days each week will you create content for next month? _____ What day next month will you schedule your content? _____ **Make a note of the days on your regular agenda. **Stick to the plan.**

Website Data: If a reader searched for you on the Internet and found your website, how could you entice them to sign up for your newsletter?

Third 30 Days

Look over tasks from the Three Month Planner and list below two to four from each project. Adjusting to new organizational habits can take time. Don't give up. Completing ten to twelve is much better than accomplishing nothing. Never stop trying.

Quarterly Goal Focus Items for Next 30 Days:

Circle the box for the four tasks that need to be done first. Move those to your first weekly action plan.

*Each week you'll review this page, check off completed tasks, circle next items, and then move them to the next weekly action plan.

Look at the items above. Do any need to be broken down further? Do you know how to handle each? Do any require outside help? Use the space below, if needed, to expand on what each task will require for you to succeed in completing it.

Monthly Planner for:_____ (which Social Media account)   Day(s) to Schedule:_____

What to post and when. Schedule ahead! Check project calendars first, then add the relevant post info below. Fill in the rest with targeted audience content, things that make you laugh, or share posts from your newsfeed that caught your attention and you think your readers might enjoy.   *Check next to day when you've scheduled the post

—> Interior columns can be used for multiple accounts, multiple posts, or ignored. Use only if needed.<—

Date	Type of Post(s)	Time	PtP
☐			
☐			
☐			
☐			
☐			
☐			
☐			
☐			
☐			
☐			
☐			
☐			
☐			
☐			
☐			
☐			
☐			
☐			
☐			
☐			
☐			
☐			
☐			
☐			
☐			
☐			
☐			
☐			
☐			

PtP = Paid to Promote

Go back and review the stats from your account. Which type of content performed the best? Highlight the top ten **non-paid** posts from the past month. Moving forward, create similar content, or expand on the theme to better reach your audience. Which posts did you **P**ay **to P**romote? Want to track the stats? Create a hand-made table on a dot-grid page of your choosing. You can do this!

Week One: ____ / ____ / ____

Top Three Focus Items from Monthly Breakdown:

Are you feeling strong? Attempt a bonus task:

☐   ☐   ☐   ☐

Weekly Action Plan: Besides your daily writing time, what else do you need to accomplish? Admin work, cover design, editing, research? Block time for focus items first, then be realistic with what you can handle daily.

"I try to create sympathy for my characters, then turn the monsters loose." —Stephen King

Date

     :   ☐

     :   ☐

     :   ☐

     :   ☐

     :   ☐

     :   ☐

Week in Review: Did you finish all the tasks? **Regroup and keep going.**

Week Two: ____ / ____ / ____

Next Three Focus Items from Monthly Breakdown:

Are you feeling strong? Attempt a bonus task:

☐   ☐   ☐   ☐

Weekly Action Plan: *Map out what needs to be done and add task to your regular weekly planner/agenda.

"If you can tell stories, create characters, devise incidents, and have sincerity and passion, it doesn't matter a damn how you write." —Somerset Maugham

Date

     :   ☐

     :   ☐

     :   ☐

     :   ☐

     :   ☐

     :   ☐

Week in Review: Read previous week's prompt and get to it!

Week Three: ____/____/____
Next Three Focus Items from Monthly Breakdown: Are you feeling strong? Attempt a bonus task:

☐   ☐   ☐   ☐

Weekly Action Plan: Wah-pesh! Snap that whip on your own ass and get to work. That book won't write itself. Dammit.

"When you have a great and difficult task, something perhaps almost impossible, if you only work a little at a time, every day a little, suddenly the work will finish itself." —Isak Dinesen

Date

: _____ ☐

: _____ ☐

: _____ ☐

: _____ ☐

: _____ ☐

: _____ ☐

: _____ ☐

Week in Review: Check, circle, highlight, cross off — whatever makes you happy when you look at the page. Do it and move forward.

Week Four: ____/____/____
Next Three Focus Items from Monthly Breakdown: Are you feeling strong? Attempt a bonus task:

☐   ☐   ☐   ☐

Weekly Action Plan: *Add the above tasks to your regular weekly planner/agenda. Learn what you can handle and then keep it up.

"It always seems impossible until it's done." —Nelson Mandela

Date

: _____ ☐

: _____ ☐

: _____ ☐

: _____ ☐

: _____ ☐

: _____ ☐

: _____ ☐

Week in Review: If you're falling way behind, you may need to adjust your month and what you can handle. Create a new plan.

Days 29-31 (as needed): _____/_____/_____

Last Focus Items from Monthly Breakdown:

☐   ☐   ☐   ☐

Weekly Action Plan: *Map out what needs to be done when and add to your regular weekly planner/agenda

"Everybody walks past a thousand story ideas every day. The good writers are the ones who see five or six of them. Most people don't see any." —Orson Scott Card

Date

_____ : _____ ☐

_____ : _____ ☐

_____ : _____ ☐

_____ : _____ ☐

_____ : _____ ☐

Quarterly Review:

What worked? Did you see an improvement to your organizational efforts? What changes do you need to make moving forward to meet your goals and dreams? How do you need to alter your day to do more? Use the area below to tweak your efforts, makes lists, or track what was achieved.

_____

_____

_____

_____

_____

_____

_____

_____

_____

_____

_____

Three Month Goal Planner

Look back over the third three months from each project plan. Transfer tasks into concrete goals. Check off when complete. Try not to over-commit and drive yourself crazy. Who needs that? Therapy is expensive.

Goal:

Project:

Due Date:

Tasks to complete this Goal:

☐ 1

☐ 2

☐ 3

☐ 4

☐ 5

☐ 6

☐ 7

Goal:

Due Date:

Tasks to complete this Goal:

☐ 1

☐ 2

☐ 3

☐ 4

☐ 5

☐ 6

☐ 7

Goal:

Project:

Due Date:

Tasks to complete this Goal:

☐ 1

☐ 2

☐ 3

☐ 4

☐ 5

☐ 6

☐ 7

Goal:

Project:

Due Date:

Tasks to complete this Goal:

☐ 1

☐ 2

☐ 3

☐ 4

☐ 5

☐ 6

☐ 7

Goal:

Project:

Due Date:

Tasks to complete this Goal:

☐ 1

☐ 2

☐ 3

☐ 4

☐ 5

☐ 6

☐ 7

Goal:

Project:

Due Date:

Tasks to complete this Goal:

☐ 1

☐ 2

☐ 3

☐ 4

☐ 5

☐ 6

☐ 7

Goal:

Project:

Due Date:

Tasks to complete this Goal:

☐ 1

☐ 2

☐ 3

☐ 4

☐ 5

☐ 6

☐ 7

Goal:

Project:

Due Date:

Tasks to complete this Goal:

☐ 1

☐ 2

☐ 3

☐ 4

☐ 5

☐ 6

☐ 7

Goal:

Project:

Due Date:

Tasks to complete this Goal:

☐ 1

☐ 2

☐ 3

☐ 4

☐ 5

☐ 6

☐ 7

Goal:

First 30 Days

Look over tasks from the Three Month Planner and list below two to four from each project.

Quarterly Goal Focus Items for Next 30 Days:

☐   ☐   ☐   ☐   ☐

☐   ☐   ☐   ☐   ☐

☐   ☐   ☐   ☐   ☐

☐   ☐   ☐   ☐   ☐

☐   ☐   ☐   ☐   ☐

Circle the box for the three tasks that need to be done first. Move those to your first weekly action plan.

*Each week you'll review this page, check off completed tasks, circle next items, and then move them to the next weekly action plan.

Look at the items above. Do any need to be broken down further? Do you know how to handle each? Do any require outside help? Use the space below, if needed, to expand on what each task will require for you to succeed in completing it.

Monthly Planner for:_____ (which Social Media account)   Day(s) to Schedule:_____

What to post and when. Schedule ahead! Check project calendars first, then add the relevant post info below. Fill in the rest with targeted audience content, things that make you laugh, or share posts from your newsfeed that caught your attention and you think your readers might enjoy.   *Check next to day when you've scheduled the post

—> Interior columns can be used for multiple accounts, multiple posts, or ignored. Use only if needed.<—

Date	Type of Post(s)			Time	PtP
☐					
☐					
☐					
☐					
☐					
☐					
☐					
☐					
☐					
☐					
☐					
☐					
☐					
☐					
☐					
☐					
☐					
☐					
☐					
☐					
☐					
☐					
☐					
☐					
☐					
☐					
☐					
☐					

PtP = Paid to Promote

Go back and review the stats from your account. Which type of content performed the best? Highlight the top ten **non-paid** posts from the past month. Moving forward, create similar content, or expand on the theme to better reach your audience. Which posts did you **P**ay **to P**romote? Want to track the stats? Create a hand-made table on a dot-grid page of your choosing. You can do this!

© Plot Your Work

Week One: _____/_____/_____

Top Three Focus Items from Monthly Breakdown:　　　　　Are you feeling strong? Attempt a bonus task:

☐　　　　　　　　☐　　　　　　　　☐　　　　　　　　☐

Weekly Action Plan: *Block time for focus items in your agenda, then be realistic with what else you can handle.

"When writing a novel a writer should create living people; people, not characters.
A character is a caricature." —Ernest Hemingway

Date

　　　　:　　　　　　　　　　　　　　　　　　　　　　　　☐

　　　　:　　　　　　　　　　　　　　　　　　　　　　　　☐

　　　　:　　　　　　　　　　　　　　　　　　　　　　　　☐

　　　　:　　　　　　　　　　　　　　　　　　　　　　　　☐

　　　　:　　　　　　　　　　　　　　　　　　　　　　　　☐

　　　　:　　　　　　　　　　　　　　　　　　　　　　　　☐

　　　　:　　　　　　　　　　　　　　　　　　　　　　　　☐

Week in Review: You've made it pretty darn far in this project planner. You know what we call writers who don't quit? **Published.**

Week Two: _____/_____/_____

Next Three Focus Items from Monthly Breakdown:　　　　　Are you feeling strong? Attempt a bonus task:

☐　　　　　　　　☐　　　　　　　　☐　　　　　　　　☐

Weekly Action Plan: Map out what needs to be done and DO IT. Check your regular agenda and remember to schedule time for **you.**

"I love deadlines. I like the whooshing sound they make as they fly by." —Douglas Adam

Date

　　　　:　　　　　　　　　　　　　　　　　　　　　　　　☐

　　　　:　　　　　　　　　　　　　　　　　　　　　　　　☐

　　　　:　　　　　　　　　　　　　　　　　　　　　　　　☐

　　　　:　　　　　　　　　　　　　　　　　　　　　　　　☐

　　　　:　　　　　　　　　　　　　　　　　　　　　　　　☐

　　　　:　　　　　　　　　　　　　　　　　　　　　　　　☐

　　　　:　　　　　　　　　　　　　　　　　　　　　　　　☐

Week in Review: Read previous week's prompt and get to it!

Week Three: _____ / _____ / _____
Next Three Focus Items from Monthly Breakdown:　　　　　Are you feeling strong? Attempt a bonus task:

☐　　　　　☐　　　　　☐　　　　　☐

Weekly Action Plan: Are you excited to work this week? You should be, it's a freakin' dream job. Even when the pay is crap.

"Success is the child of drudgery and perseverance. It cannot be coaxed or bribed;
pay the price and it is yours." —Orison Swett Marden

Date

:　　　　　☐

:　　　　　☐

:　　　　　☐

:　　　　　☐

:　　　　　☐

:　　　　　☐

:　　　　　☐

Week in Review: Circle unfinished tasks and move to next week. Make time to complete them in addition to the ones you'll have for the upcoming week.

Week Four: _____ / _____ / _____
Next Three Focus Items from Monthly Breakdown:　　　　　Are you feeling strong? Attempt a bonus task:

☐　　　　　☐　　　　　☐　　　　　☐

Weekly Action Plan: *Add to your regular weekly planner/agenda.

"A river cuts through rock, not because of its power, but because of its persistence." —Jim Watkins

Date

:　　　　　☐

:　　　　　☐

:　　　　　☐

:　　　　　☐

:　　　　　☐

:　　　　　☐

:　　　　　☐

Week in Review: Check off what you did, circle and move what you didn't, and plan next week's tasks. You got this.

　　　　　© **Plot Your Work**

Days 29-31 (as needed): _____/_____/_____

Last Focus Items from Monthly Breakdown:

☐	☐	☐	☐

Weekly Action Plan: *Map out what needs to be done when and add to your regular weekly planner/agenda

> *"Tell the readers a story! Because without a story, you are merely using words to prove you can string them together in logical sentences."* —Anne McCaffrey

Date

:   ☐

:   ☐

:   ☐

:   ☐

:   ☐

Month in Review: You know what to do by now, right? Track what you're doing, pat yourself on the back, and celebrate the accomplishments so you're more inclined to repeat the effort. If you're a parent, you know how to manipulate your kids. Use that same crap on yourself, seriously. Whatever it takes!

What can you do to help yourself succeed? Get up early, hire help, or outline better so your writing time is more fruitful. Excuses will get you the same results you had in the past, and isn't the point to improve as we move forward?

Newsletter: Day and Time of last newsletter: _____ Day One Open Rate: _____ Day Five, Total Open Rate:_____
Did you cross-post your newsletter to social media? Your newsletter is only a valuable marketing tool if people READ IT

Social Media: Total # of Scheduled Posts: _____ Total # of Live Posts: _____ Total Reach for Month: _____
What type of posts had the most views? The most likes and comments? Go back and highlight them in your Social Media Planning section for this month. What days each week will you create content for next month? _____ What day next month will you schedule your content? _____ **Make a note of the days on your regular agenda. **Stick to the plan.**

Website Data: Use this area to track data regarding your website, or use it as a place to make note on what to update:

Second 30 Days

Look over tasks from your Three Month Planner and list below two to four from each project.

Quarterly Goal Focus Items for Next 30 Days:

☐   ☐   ☐   ☐   ☐

☐   ☐   ☐   ☐   ☐

☐   ☐   ☐   ☐   ☐

☐   ☐   ☐   ☐   ☐

☐   ☐   ☐   ☐   ☐

Circle the box for the three tasks that need to be done first. Move those to your first weekly action plan.

*Each week you'll review this page, check off completed tasks, circle next items, and then move them to the next weekly action plan.

Look at the items above. Do any need to be broken down further? Do you know how to handle each? Do any require outside help? Use the space below, if needed, to expand on what each task will require for you to succeed in completing it.

Monthly Planner for:_____ (which Social Media account)   Day(s) to Schedule:_____

What to post and when. Schedule ahead! Check project calendars first, then add the relevant post info below. Fill in the rest with targeted audience content, things that make you laugh, or share posts from your newsfeed that caught your attention and you think your readers might enjoy.   *Check next to day when you've scheduled the post

—> Interior columns can be used for multiple accounts, multiple posts, or ignored. Use only if needed.<—

Date	Type of Post(s)			Time	PtP
☐					
☐					
☐					
☐					
☐					
☐					
☐					
☐					
☐					
☐					
☐					
☐					
☐					
☐					
☐					
☐					
☐					
☐					
☐					
☐					
☐					
☐					
☐					
☐					
☐					
☐					
☐					
☐					
☐					

PtP = Paid to Promote

Go back and review the stats from your account. Which type of content performed the best? Highlight the top ten **non-paid** posts from the past month. Moving forward, create similar content, or expand on the theme to better reach your audience. Which posts did you **P**ay **t**o **P**romote? Want to track the stats? Create a hand-made table on a dot-grid page of your choosing. You can do this!

© Plot Your Work

Week One: ____/____/____

Top Three Focus Items from Monthly Breakdown: Are you feeling strong? Attempt a bonus task:

☐   ☐   ☐   ☐

Weekly Action Plan: Do all the things! Consume copious cups of coffee if necessary.

"Success is the sum of small efforts, repeated day in and day out." —Robert Collier

Date

:   ☐

:   ☐

:   ☐

:   ☐

:   ☐

:   ☐

Week in Review: Month four! Don't give up now. **Regroup and keep going.**

Week Two: ____/____/____

Next Three Focus Items from Monthly Breakdown: Are you feeling strong? Attempt a bonus task:

☐   ☐   ☐   ☐

Weekly Action Plan: Plan, plot, map it out—whatever you need. Check your agenda and remember to schedule time for **you.**

"Perseverance is not a long race; it is many short races one after the other." —Walter Elliot

Date

:   ☐

:   ☐

:   ☐

:   ☐

:   ☐

:   ☐

Week in Review: Read previous week's prompt and get to it!

Week Three: _____/_____/_____

Next Three Focus Items from Monthly Breakdown: Are you feeling strong? Attempt a bonus task:

☐   ☐   ☐   ☐

Weekly Action Plan: *Add to your regular weekly planner/agenda.

"Never confuse a single defeat with a final defeat." —F. Scott Fitzgerald

Date

_____:_____   ☐

_____:_____   ☐

_____:_____   ☐

_____:_____   ☐

_____:_____   ☐

_____:_____   ☐

_____:_____   ☐

Week in Review: Check, circle, mark it off! You've done something this week. Celebrate it, no matter how small.

Week Four: _____/_____/_____

Next Three Focus Items from Monthly Breakdown: Are you feeling strong? Attempt a bonus task:

☐   ☐   ☐   ☐

Weekly Action Plan: *Add to your regular weekly planner/agenda.

"It is the writer who might catch the imagination of young people, and plant a seed that will flower and come to fruition." —Isaac Asimov

Date

_____:_____   ☐

_____:_____   ☐

_____:_____   ☐

_____:_____   ☐

_____:_____   ☐

_____:_____   ☐

_____:_____   ☐

Week in Review: Check off what you did, circle and move what you didn't, and plan next week's tasks. You got this.

Days 29-31 (as needed): _____/_____/_____

Last Focus Items from Monthly Breakdown:

☐   ☐   ☐   ☐

Weekly Action Plan: *Map out what needs to be done when and add to your regular weekly planner/agenda

"Writing a book is a horrible, exhausting struggle, like a long bout of some painful illness. One would never undertake such a thing if one were not driven on by some demon whom one can neither resist nor understand." —George Orwell

Date

_____ : _____ ☐

_____ : _____ ☐

_____ : _____ ☐

_____ : _____ ☐

_____ : _____ ☐

Month in Review: Are you consistently meeting your tasks each week? Amp things up in your next month. **Are you falling behind and getting stressed?** Map out a new plan. Try, try again. Never quit!

What can you do to help yourself succeed? Get up early, hire help, outline better so your writing time is more fruitful. Excuses will get you the same results you had in the past, and isn't the point to improve as we move forward?

Newsletter: When was your newsletter sent?: Day and Time: _____ Day One Open Rate: _____ Day Five, Total Open Rate:_____ How can you increase your open rate? Offer a sale? Run a contest? Big numbers on a list don't mean squat if those numbers don't equate to people who OPEN and READ. Newsletter content for next month:

_____

_____

_____

Social Media: Total # of Scheduled Posts: _____ Total # of Live Posts: _____ Total Reach for Month: _____ What type of posts had the most views? The most likes and comments? Go back and highlight them in your Social Media Planning section for this month. What days each week will you create content for next month? _____ What day next month will you schedule your content? _____ **Make a note of the days on your regular agenda. Stick to the plan.**

Website Data:

_____

_____

_____

_____

_____

_____

© **Plot Your Work**

Third 30 Days

Look over tasks from the Three Month Planner, and list below three to six from each project.

Quarterly Goal Focus Items for Next 30 Days:

☐	☐	☐	☐	☐
☐	☐	☐	☐	☐
☐	☐	☐	☐	☐
☐	☐	☐	☐	☐
☐	☐	☐	☐	☐

Circle the box for the four tasks that need to be done first. Move those to your first weekly action plan.

*Each week you'll review this page, check off completed tasks, circle next items, and then move them to the next weekly action plan.

Look at the items above. Do any need to be broken down further? Do you know how to handle each? Do any require outside help? Use the space below, if needed, to expand on what each task will require for you to succeed in completing it.

Monthly Planner for:_____ (which Social Media account)   Day(s) to Schedule:_____

What to post and when. Schedule ahead! Check project calendars first, then add the relevant post info below. Fill in the rest with targeted audience content, things that make you laugh, or share posts from your newsfeed that caught your attention and you think your readers might enjoy.   *Check next to day when you've scheduled the post

—> Interior columns can be used for multiple accounts, multiple posts, or ignored. Use only if needed.<—

Date	Type of Post(s)	Time	PtP
☐			
☐			
☐			
☐			
☐			
☐			
☐			
☐			
☐			
☐			
☐			
☐			
☐			
☐			
☐			
☐			
☐			
☐			
☐			
☐			
☐			
☐			
☐			
☐			
☐			
☐			
☐			
☐			
☐			
☐			
☐			

PtP = Paid to Promote

Go back and review the stats from your account. Which type of content performed the best? Highlight the top ten **non-paid** posts from the past month. Moving forward, create similar content, or expand on the theme to better reach your audience. Which posts did you **P**ay **to P**romote? Want to track the stats? Create a hand-made table on a dot-grid page of your choosing. You can do this!

© **Plot Your Work**

Week One: ____/____/____

Top Three Focus Items from Monthly Breakdown:

Are you feeling strong? Attempt a bonus task:

☐　　　　　　　☐　　　　　　　☐　　　　☐

Weekly Action Plan: Make a list, figure out what needs to be done, and divide it among the days below. Be realistic. Stay sane.

"Most of the basic material a writer works with is acquired before the age of fifteen." —Willa Cather

Date

. : ☐

. : ☐

. : ☐

. : ☐

. : ☐

. : ☐

. : ☐

<u>**Week in Review:**</u> Report! What's done, what's not? Make yourself accountable.

Week Two: ____/____/____

Next Three Focus Items from Monthly Breakdown:

Are you feeling strong? Attempt a bonus task:

☐　　　　　　　☐　　　　　　　☐　　　　☐

Weekly Action Plan: *Map out what needs to be done and add to your regular weekly planner/agenda. Block time for focus items first, then be realistic with what else you can handle daily. Check your regular agenda and remember to schedule time for **you.**

"All the information you need can be given in dialogue." —Elmore Leonard

Date

. : ☐

. : ☐

. : ☐

. : ☐

. : ☐

. : ☐

. : ☐

<u>**Week in Review:**</u> The only way to succeed is to stick to a plan and keep at it, even when you have set backs, sick days, and personal issues. Don't give up.

Week Three: _____/_____/_____
Next Three Focus Items from Monthly Breakdown: Are you feeling strong? Attempt a bonus task:

☐   ☐   ☐   ☐

Weekly Action Plan: *Add to your regular weekly planner/agenda.

"There's no such thing as writer's block. That was invented by people in California who couldn't write." —Terry Pratchet

Date

: _____ ☐
: _____ ☐
: _____ ☐
: _____ ☐
: _____ ☐
: _____ ☐
: _____ ☐

Week in Review: Check, circle, move, plan more. To stop means your work stagnates. Don't start rotting. Keep moving.

Week Four: _____/_____/_____
Next Three Focus Items from Monthly Breakdown: Are you feeling strong? Attempt a bonus task:

☐   ☐   ☐   ☐

Weekly Action Plan: *Add to your regular weekly planner/agenda.

"A failure is not always a mistake. It may simply be the best one can do under the circumstances. The real mistake is to stop trying." —B. F. Skinner

Date

: _____ ☐
: _____ ☐
: _____ ☐
: _____ ☐
: _____ ☐
: _____ ☐
: _____ ☐

Week in Review: Check off what you did, circle and move what you didn't, and plan next week's tasks. You got this.

Days 29-31 (as needed): _____ / _____ / _____

Last Focus Items from Monthly Breakdown:

☐   ☐   ☐   ☐

Weekly Action Plan: *Map out what needs to be done when and add to your regular weekly planner/agenda

"Courage doesn't always roar, sometimes it's the quiet voice at the end of the day whispering I will try again tomorrow." —Mary Anne Radmacher

Date

_____ :_____   ☐

_____ :_____   ☐

_____ :_____   ☐

_____ :_____   ☐

Quarterly Review:

What worked? Did you see an improvement to your organizational efforts? What changes do you need to make moving forward to meet your goals and dreams?

Three Month Goal Planner
Look back over the last three months from each project plan. Transfer tasks into concrete goals. Check off when complete. You ready to amp it up and need more sheets? Check out our website for extra sheets.

Goal:

Project:

Due Date:

Tasks to complete this Goal:

☐ 1

☐ 2

☐ 3

☐ 4

☐ 5

☐ 6

☐ 7

Goal:

Project:

Due Date:

Tasks to complete this Goal:

☐ 1

☐ 2

☐ 3

☐ 4

☐ 5

☐ 6

☐ 7

Goal:

Project:

Due Date:

Tasks to complete this Goal:

☐ 1

☐ 2

☐ 3

☐ 4

☐ 5

☐ 6

☐ 7

Goal:

Project:

Due Date:

Tasks to complete this Goal:

☐ 1

☐ 2

☐ 3

☐ 4

☐ 5

☐ 6

☐ 7

Goal:

Project:

Due Date:

Tasks to complete this Goal:

☐ 1

☐ 2

☐ 3

☐ 4

☐ 5

☐ 6

☐ 7

Goal:

Project:

Due Date:

Tasks to complete this Goal:

☐ 1

☐ 2

☐ 3

☐ 4

☐ 5

☐ 6

☐ 7

Goal:

Project:

Due Date:

Tasks to complete this Goal:

☐ 1

☐ 2

☐ 3

☐ 4

☐ 5

☐ 6

☐ 7

Goal:

Project:

Due Date:

Tasks to complete this Goal:

☐ 1

☐ 2

☐ 3

☐ 4

☐ 5

☐ 6

☐ 7

Goal:

Project:

Due Date:

Tasks to complete this Goal:

☐ 1

☐ 2

☐ 3

☐ 4

☐ 5

☐ 6

☐ 7

First 30 Days

Look over tasks from the Three Month Planner and list below one to three (or more!) from each project.

Quarterly Goal Focus Items for Next 30 Days:

☐	☐	☐	☐	☐
☐	☐	☐	☐	☐
☐	☐	☐	☐	☐
☐	☐	☐	☐	☐
☐	☐	☐	☐	☐

Circle the box for the three tasks that need to be done first. Move those to your first weekly action plan.

*Each week you'll review this page, check off completed tasks, circle next items, and then move them to the next weekly action plan.

Look at the items above. Do any need to be broken down further? Do you know how to handle each? Do any require outside help? Use the space below, if needed, to expand on what each task will require for you to succeed in completing it.

....

....

....

....

....

....

....

....

....

....

Monthly Planner for:_____ (which Social Media account)   Day(s) to Schedule:_____

What to post and when. Schedule ahead! Check project calendars first, then add the relevant post info below. Fill in the rest with targeted audience content, things that make you laugh, or share posts from your newsfeed that caught your attention and you think your readers might enjoy.   *Check next to day when you've scheduled the post

—> Interior columns can be used for multiple accounts, multiple posts, or ignored. Use only if needed.<—

Date	Type of Post(s)	Time	PtP
☐			
☐			
☐			
☐			
☐			
☐			
☐			
☐			
☐			
☐			
☐			
☐			
☐			
☐			
☐			
☐			
☐			
☐			
☐			
☐			
☐			
☐			
☐			
☐			
☐			
☐			
☐			
☐			
☐			
☐			

PtP = Paid to Promote

Go back and review the stats from your account. Which type of content performed the best? Highlight the top ten **non-paid** posts from the past month. Moving forward, create similar content, or expand on the theme to better reach your audience. Which posts did you **P**ay **to P**romote? Want to track the stats? Create a hand-made table on a dot-grid page of your choosing. You can do this!

Week One: ____/____/____

Top Three Focus Items from Monthly Breakdown:

Are you feeling strong? Attempt a bonus task:

☐   ☐   ☐   ☐

Weekly Action Plan: Plan your work and work your plan. Yup, that's what the name of this product was based on. For reals.

"Almost anyone can be an author; the business is to collect money and fame from this state of being." —A. A. Milne

Date

:   ☐

:   ☐

:   ☐

:   ☐

:   ☐

:   ☐

:   ☐

Week in Review: It's the start of the last quarter. You've come a long way, baby! You know what to do, these prompts are just to make you smile.

Week Two: ____/____/____

Next Three Focus Items from Monthly Breakdown:

Are you feeling strong? Attempt a bonus task:

☐   ☐   ☐   ☐

Weekly Action Plan: *Add to your regular weekly planner/agenda. Block time for focus items first, then be realistic with what else you can handle daily. Check your regular agenda and remember to schedule time for **you.**

"It does not matter how slowly you go as long as you do not stop." —Confucius

Date

:   ☐

:   ☐

:   ☐

:   ☐

:   ☐

:   ☐

:   ☐

Week in Review: What worked and what didn't? Only you can decide what you should keep doing and what you need to stop.

Week Three: ____/____/____

Next Three Focus Items from Monthly Breakdown:

Are you feeling strong? Attempt a bonus task:

☐   ☐   ☐   ☐

Weekly Action Plan: Accountability isn't just a word. Live it. Take control of what you need to do. And then DO IT.

"Literature is all, or mostly, about sex." —Anthony Burgess

Date

:   ☐

:   ☐

:   ☐

:   ☐

:   ☐

:   ☐

:   ☐

Week in Review: Instead of Reduce Reuse and Recycle, sing Check, Circle, and Move! No alliteration, but who cares?

Week Four: ____/____/____

Next Three Focus Items from Monthly Breakdown:

Are you feeling strong? Attempt a bonus task:

☐   ☐   ☐   ☐

Weekly Action Plan: *Add to your regular weekly planner/agenda.

"Courage is not having the strength to go on; it is going on when you don't have the strength." —Theodore Roosevelt

Date

:   ☐

:   ☐

:   ☐

:   ☐

:   ☐

:   ☐

:   ☐

Week in Review: Check off what you did, circle and move what you didn't, and plan next week's tasks. You got this.

Days 29-31 (as needed): _____/_____/_____

Last Focus Items from Monthly Breakdown:

☐   ☐   ☐   ☐

Weekly Action Plan: *Map out what needs to be done when and add tasks to your regular weekly planner/agenda

"If it sounds like writing, I rewrite it. Or, if proper usage gets in the way, it may have to go. I can't allow what we learned in English composition to disrupt the sound and rhythm of the narrative." —Elmore Leonard

Date

        :   ☐

        :   ☐

        :   ☐

        :   ☐

        :   ☐

Month in Review: *Remember:* The goal in using this planner is to succeed in all your projects, not to make yourself feel inadequate. If everything you wanted to accomplish didn't happen, learn from it. Alter your habits moving forward. Adjust your expectations. Or, give yourself the kick in the ass you need to finally **actualize** your dreams. It's your choice. It always has been.

Newsletter: Date and Time: _____ Day One Open Rate: _____ Day Five, Total Open Rate:_____ Content for next month:

Social Media: Total # of Scheduled Posts: _____ Total # of Live Posts: _____ Total Reach for Month: _____ What type of posts had the most views? The most likes and comments? Go back and highlight them in your Social Media Planning section for this month. What days each week will you create content for next month? _____ What day next month will you schedule your content? _____ **Make a note of the days on your regular agenda. Stick to the plan.**

Website Data:

Second 30 Days

Look over tasks from your Three Month Planner and list below three to six from each project.

Quarterly Goal Focus Items for Next 30 Days:

☐   ☐   ☐   ☐   ☐

☐   ☐   ☐   ☐   ☐

☐   ☐   ☐   ☐   ☐

☐   ☐   ☐   ☐   ☐

☐   ☐   ☐   ☐   ☐

Circle the box for the three tasks that need to be done first. Move those to your first weekly action plan.

*Each week you'll review this page, check off completed tasks, circle next items, and then move them to the next weekly action plan.

Look at the items above. Do any need to be broken down further? Do you know how to handle each? Do any require outside help? Use the space below, if needed, to expand on what each task will require for you to succeed in completing it.

Monthly Planner for:_____ (which Social Media account)   Day(s) to Schedule:_____

What to post and when. Schedule ahead! Check project calendars first, then add the relevant post info below. Fill in the rest with targeted audience content, things that make you laugh, or share posts from your newsfeed that caught your attention and you think your readers might enjoy.   *Check next to day when you've scheduled the post

—> Interior columns can be used for multiple accounts, multiple posts, or ignored. Use only if needed.<—

Date	Type of Post(s)			Time	PtP
☐					
☐					
☐					
☐					
☐					
☐					
☐					
☐					
☐					
☐					
☐					
☐					
☐					
☐					
☐					
☐					
☐					
☐					
☐					
☐					
☐					
☐					
☐					
☐					
☐					
☐					
☐					
☐					

PtP = Paid to Promote

Go back and review the stats from your account. Which type of content performed the best? Highlight the top ten **non-paid** posts from the past month. Moving forward, create similar content, or expand on the theme to better reach your audience. Which posts did you **P**ay **to P**romote? Want to track the stats? Create a hand-made table on a dot-grid page of your choosing. You can do this!

© **Plot Your Work**

Week One: _____/_____/_____

Top Three Focus Items from Monthly Breakdown: Are you feeling strong? Attempt a bonus task:

☐   ☐   ☐   ☐

Weekly Action Plan: Block time for focus items first, then be realistic with what you can handle.

"I went for years not finishing anything. Because, of course, when you finish something you can be judged." —Erica Jong

Date

:   ☐

:   ☐

:   ☐

:   ☐

:   ☐

:   ☐

:   ☐

Week in Review: How is the plan coming along? Everything running smoothly? If not, decide what needs fixing and fix it.

Week Two: _____/_____/_____

Next Three Focus Items from Monthly Breakdown: Are you feeling strong? Attempt a bonus task:

☐   ☐   ☐   ☐

Weekly Action Plan: Map out what needs to be done and DO IT. Check your regular agenda and remember to schedule time for you.

"When writing a novel a writer should create living people; people, not characters.
A character is a caricature." —Ernest Hemingway

Date

:   ☐

:   ☐

:   ☐

:   ☐

:   ☐

:   ☐

:   ☐

Week in Review: Check, circle, and move! (Sung to the tune of Reduce, Reuse and Recycle) ;-)

Week Three: _____/_____/_____

Next Three Focus Items from Monthly Breakdown:

Are you feeling strong? Attempt a bonus task:

☐   ☐   ☐   ☐

Weekly Action Plan: Circle unfinished tasks and move to next week. Make time to complete them in addition to the ones you'll have for the upcoming week. If you're falling way behind already, you may need to adjust your month and what you can handle.
Regroup and keep going.

Date

: .... ☐

: .... ☐

: .... ☐

: .... ☐

: .... ☐

: .... ☐

Week in Review: Circle unfinished tasks and move to next week. Make time to complete them in addition to the ones you'll have for the upcoming week.

Week Four: _____/_____/_____

Next Three Focus Items from Monthly Breakdown:

Are you feeling strong? Attempt a bonus task:

☐   ☐   ☐   ☐

Weekly Action Plan: Transfer tasks to your regular planner or agenda.

Date

: .... ☐

: .... ☐

: .... ☐

: .... ☐

: .... ☐

: .... ☐

"Perseverance is the hard work you do after you get tired of doing the hard work you already did." —Newt Gingrich

Week in Review: Check off what you did, circle and move what you didn't, and plan next week's tasks. You got this.

© **Plot Your Work**

Days 29-31 (as needed): _____/_____/_____

Last Focus Items from Monthly Breakdown:

☐   ☐   ☐   ☐

Weekly Action Plan: *Map out what needs to be done when and add to your regular weekly planner/agenda

"Develop success from failures. Discouragement and failure are two of the surest stepping stones to success." —Dale Carnegie

Date

    : ....

.... ☐

    : ....

.... ☐

    : ....

.... ☐

    : ....

.... ☐

    : ....

.... ☐

Month in Review: **You've been at this for a while now. Is the project planner helping you to realize your writing goals? If yes, we'd like to hear from you!** You can find us online at www.plotyourwork.com, or on Facebook under our Page by the same name. If you have suggestions for improvement on this product, please share! It's a continually evolving work in progress. Kind of like your first crappy manuscript.

Newsletter: Date and Time: _____ Day One Open Rate: _____ Day Five, Total Open Rate:_____ Content for next month's newsletter:

....

....

....

....

Social Media: Total # of Scheduled Posts: _____ Total # of Live Posts: _____ Total Reach for Month: _____ What type of posts had the most views? The most likes and comments? Go back and highlight them in your Social Media Planning section for this month. What days each week will you create content for next month? _____ What day next month will you schedule your content? _____ **Make a note of the days on your regular agenda. Stick to the plan.**

Website Data:

....

....

....

....

....

....

....

Third 30 Days

Look over tasks from the Three Month Planner and list below three to six from each project.

Quarterly Goal Focus Items for Next 30 Days:

☐   ☐   ☐   ☐   ☐

☐   ☐   ☐   ☐   ☐

☐   ☐   ☐   ☐   ☐

☐   ☐   ☐   ☐   ☐

☐   ☐   ☐   ☐   ☐

Circle the box for the four tasks that need to be done first. Move those to your first weekly action plan.

*Each week you'll review this page, check off completed tasks, circle next items, and then move them to the next weekly action plan.

Look at the items above. Do any need to be broken down further? Do you know how to handle each? Do any require outside help? Use the space below, if needed, to expand on what each task will require for you to succeed in completing it.

....

....

....

....

....

....

....

....

....

....

Monthly Planner for:_____ (which Social Media account)   Day(s) to Schedule:_____

What to post and when. Schedule ahead! Check project calendars first, then add the relevant post info below. Fill in the rest with targeted audience content, things that make you laugh, or share posts from your newsfeed that caught your attention and you think your readers might enjoy.   *Check next to day when you've scheduled the post

—> Interior columns can be used for multiple accounts, multiple posts, or ignored. Use only if needed.<—

Date	Type of Post(s)			Time	PtP
☐					
☐					
☐					
☐					
☐					
☐					
☐					
☐					
☐					
☐					
☐					
☐					
☐					
☐					
☐					
☐					
☐					
☐					
☐					
☐					
☐					
☐					
☐					
☐					
☐					
☐					
☐					
☐					
☐					
☐					
☐					

PtP = Paid to Promote

Go back and review the stats from your account. Which type of content performed the best? Highlight the top ten **non-paid** posts from the past month. Moving forward, create similar content, or expand on the theme to better reach your audience. Which posts did you **P**ay **to P**romote? Want to track the stats? Create a hand-made table on a dot-grid page of your choosing. You can do this!

Week One: _____/_____/_____

Top Three Focus Items from Monthly Breakdown: Are you feeling strong? Attempt a bonus task:

☐   ☐   ☐   ☐

Weekly Action Plan: Make a list, figure out what needs to be done, and divide it among the days below. Be realistic. Stay sane.

"I don't know the key to success, but the key to failure is trying to please everybody." —Bill Cosby

Date

⋮   ☐

⋮   ☐

⋮   ☐

⋮   ☐

⋮   ☐

⋮   ☐

⋮   ☐

Week in Review: Report! What's done, what's not? Make yourself accountable.

Week Two: _____/_____/_____

Next Three Focus Items from Monthly Breakdown: Are you feeling strong? Attempt a bonus task:

☐   ☐   ☐   ☐

Weekly Action Plan: *Map out what needs to be done and add to your regular weekly planner/agenda.

"Write drunk, edit sober." —Ernest Hemingway

Date

⋮   ☐

⋮   ☐

⋮   ☐

⋮   ☐

⋮   ☐

⋮   ☐

⋮   ☐

Week in Review: The only way to succeed is to stick to a plan and keep at it, even when you have set backs, sick days, and

Week Three: _____/_____/_____
Next Three Focus Items from Monthly Breakdown:

Are you feeling strong? Attempt a bonus task:

☐   ☐   ☐   ☐

Weekly Action Plan: *Add to your regular weekly planner/agenda.

"There is only one plot—things are not what they seem." Jim Thompson

Date

: .... ☐

: .... ☐

: .... ☐

: .... ☐

: .... ☐

: .... ☐

:

Week in Review: Check, circle, move, plan more. To stop means your work stagnates. Don't start rotting. Keep moving.

Week Four: _____/_____/_____
Next Three Focus Items from Monthly Breakdown:

Are you feeling strong? Attempt a bonus task:

☐   ☐   ☐   ☐

Weekly Action Plan: *Add to your regular weekly planner/agenda.

"Fiction is about stuff that's screwed up." Nancy Kress

Date

: .... ☐

: .... ☐

: .... ☐

: .... ☐

: .... ☐

: .... ☐

: ☐

Week in Review: Check off what you did, circle and move what you didn't, and plan next week's tasks. You got this.

Days 29-31 (as needed): _____ / _____ / _____

Last Focus Items from Monthly Breakdown:

☐   ☐   ☐   ☐

Weekly Action Plan: *Map out what needs to be done when and add to your regular weekly planner/agenda

"Substitute 'damn' every time you're inclined to write 'very'; your editor will delete it and the writing will be just as it should be." —Mark Twain

Date

:   ☐

:   ☐

:   ☐

:   ☐

:   ☐

Quarterly Review:

End of the planner! So what's the verdict? Would you try this planner again? Please reach out and let us know.